BST **ACPL ITEM**
DISCARDED

The Power of Humor
at the Workplace

D1738645

The Power of Humor at the Workplace

K. Sathyanarayana

Response
Business books from SAGE
Los Angeles ■ London ■ New Delhi ■ Singapore
www.sagepublications.com

Copyright © K. Sathyanarayana, 2007

All rights reserved. No part of this book may be reproduced or utilized in any form or by any means, electronic or mechanical, including photocopying, recording or by any information storage or retrieval system, without permission in writing from the publisher.

First published in 2007 by

Response Books
Business books from SAGE
B1/I1, Mohan Cooperative Industrial Area
Mathura Road, New Delhi 110 044

Sage Publications Inc
2455 Teller Road
Thousand Oaks, California 91320

Sage Publications Ltd
1 Oliver's Yard, 55 City Road
London EC1Y 1SP

Sage Publications Asia–Pacific Pte Ltd
33 Pekin Street
#02-01 Far East Square
Singapore 048763

Published by Vivek Mehra for Response Books, typeset in 11/13.5pt Bemboo by Star Compugraphics Private Limited, Delhi and printed at Chaman Enterprises, New Delhi.

Library of Congress Cataloging-in-Publication Data

Sathyanarayana, K., 1936–
   The power of humor at the workplace/K. Sathyanarayana.
      p. cm.
   Includes bibliographical references.
1. Humor in the workplace.   I. Title.

HF5549.5.H85S28   658.4'5—dc22   2007   2007038190

ISBN: 978-0-7619-3599-5 (PB)   978-81-7829-762-0 (India-PB)

The Sage Team: Leela Kirloskar and Neha Kohli

To my good friend and a great teacher,
Professor B.H. Agalgatti, Ph.D.

Contents

List of Figures

Foreword

Humor helps everyone to go home from the workplace in a happy mood. This is a very important requirement (even though it gets neglected very often); otherwise one will be carrying the after-effects of events at the workplace to his home. As a corollary, no person will be successful if he brings domestic problems to the workplace, his mind acting as a godown of problems, worries and anxiety. By any stretch of imagination, it is very difficult to believe that such a person could be effective to his full potential. An even more dangerous feature is that this tendency can go on worsening day after day; it doesn't have any self-correcting possibility. I've found that Sense of Humor at the workplace is a very effective antidote to this vicious phenomenon. It helps in tackling problems of all types in such a way that they do not leave any residual precipitate of tension and distress.

Laughing at oneself is the most enjoyable and rewarding of all types of laughter. We need not strain ourselves too much in search of the subject matter! Our own experiences, right from our childhood days, provide ample material to narrate to others humorously and to laugh at ourselves. Listeners will join the laughter because everyone likes to laugh.

When I recall my schooldays, I cannot help mentioning how the Hindi Language was my stumbling block. I could manage to pass in only four of the 15 exams I faced. Our school principal was magnanimous in mercifully predicting: "This boy's poor Hindi will not come in the way of his rising in life."

So all my mispronunciations, poor grammar, meagre vocabulary got condoned; fortunately I could also scrape through in my S.S.C exam with just Divine help!

My mother who hailed from Nagpur was sometimes distressed that her son was weak in Hindi. She used to help me by giving special coaching at home. Once I was asked to write the summary of the lesson "*Dakiyaki Aatmakatha.*" When I finished writing, my mother asked me to read it in the presence of many relatives. When I was halfway through, my aunt asked: "Whose *aatmakatha* is this: *Dakiya ki ya Daku ki?*"

I am quite-happy that I could make all the people laugh in spite of my weak Hindi.

When my son was about five years of age, he saw a burial take place on a television serial. He had been told that when anyone passes away, he becomes united with the Almighty, who sits in His throne up above the skies. But when the corpse was lowered into a pit 5 ft below ground level he was puzzled. So he asked my wife how this poor person was going to meet God when he was being lowered 5 ft below the ground!

A sense of humor enables us to have a fresh look at what we do as a routine. This reminds me of how this step led to an interesting result, when our company was dealing with one of our overseas customers. This septuagenarian was very good in pushing his demands regarding better quality, earlier delivery, and higher discounts. Our company did its best in trying to meet each of his demands. Once he hurriedly came down to Pune, but as that day happened to be an election day in our city, we had declared a general holiday. Still we hastily arranged a meeting of the concerned persons to discuss our guest's requirements. He said in that meeting that we should double our supplies to him. I told him that this called for expansion of the manufacturing facilities; we would happily do this provided that he could assure his demand at the increased level for at least three years. He readily agreed to this condition.

Next morning when the minutes of the meeting were presented to him for his endorsement, he said that he had been brainwashed by me the earlier day to agree to some uncalled for and impossible conditions. He refused to accept our terms and said that he would immediately go back to his country. For a change I had decided to be firm, which our guest thought was impossible. I offered no objections and instead agreed to make the necessary arrangements for his road journey to Mumbai for his onward flight from India. He was informed that a boxed lunch was prepared, the hotel bill was presented and a car had been made ready. He was shocked that we did not leave him any chance to come to a compromise. He had to leave our place in a huff. When he reached Mumbai, he had fully realized that he had played his hand too dramatically. He telephoned my grandfather and apologized for his behavior. In turn my grandfather advised him that it was high time for him to hand over the reins of his enterprise to his son. That way his son would get a higher responsibility and grow into the job while he was around whenever required. To the surprise of us all, very soon, he did hand over the charge of his company to his son. He also confided to my grandfather that it was the best advice he had in his lifetime!

There is great sense in being happy at the workplace. A person can excel in his work only when he's happy. This is true regarding all types of work and is applicable to all kinds of people. When we observe children, it's easy to see them in their happiest mood when they are given a free hand to do what they like most. Adults are no exception to this universal principle.

I've found Sathyanarayana's book, "The Power of Humor at the Workplace," very interesting, useful and valuable. It could be called "Humor for Dummies." It's very educative; yet it takes a firm grip of the reader's attention and interest. The six levels of Sense of Humor described herein help the reader to evaluate himself; the several guidelines and exercises described make it easy for him to improve his sense of humor. The hundreds of well-chosen and articulated pieces of humor enable him to get initiated on the journey towards a higher sense of humor. Finally, such a person with the "Armor of Humor" is a big asset not only to the enterprise, but also to his family and society. The chapter on "Putting Humor on Agenda," is particularly helpful to the heads of organizations in reaping the benefits of Humor.

Sanjay Kirloskar
Chairman and Managing Director
Kirloskar Brothers Ltd.

Preface

This book is neither about making speeches nor about reciting jokes and funny stories to make people laugh. It is a book which is a great deal more useful and more indispensable, because it discusses "Sense of Humor" and describes the several applications of Humor as a powerful management tool.

Humor, when properly used, is well known as being an effective tool to gain attention, create rapport, and make a message more memorable. It relieves tensions, enhances relationships, motivates people, and resolves issues when other techniques fail to set them right. The benefits of Humor can be reaped in every function of management of every type of business, and the manager who is armed with a Sense of Humor enjoys an explicit edge over others at the workplace.

This book is an appeal to the corporate top management that they give due recognition to Humor at the workplace, in the same way they treat Quality, Flexibility, and Timeliness as important.

Sense of Humor, as denoted in this book includes, in addition to telling funny stories and making people laugh, many more highly rewarding traits: the ability to hold a mirror to oneself and laugh over self-made errors, silly mistakes, and blunders; the ability to laugh at the adversities and misfortunes that are part of life; the ability to persevere toward self-fulfillment; the ability to be calm and relaxed when tensions mount; to accept oneself for what one is and similarly accept the people around for who they are; the ability to achieve lofty goals as a team; to not be carried away by one's own achievements; and the generosity to admire the contributions of others with gratitude. This is a very long list. A number of eminent personalities have set before us their examples of this Sense of Humor. Their acts make us smile, chuckle, laugh, and wonder; they make us happy, surprised, envious, thoughtful, proud, and motivated. Hundreds of anecdotes, quotes, stories, jokes, observations, definitions and the like are included in this book to demonstrate the forcefulness of Humor.

Another important aim of this book is to raise a voice against the myth that Humor is an inborn gift bestowed on only a select few and hence everyone cannot hope to use Humor. *This book emphasizes that everyone, who has at anytime laughed or smiled, has a dormant Sense of Humor, which can be improved and made to blossom. It provides step-by-step guidelines to achieve this goal with a number of exercises to make those Humor muscles grow big and strong.*

The several forms of Humor are described with examples throughout the book. The reader is invited to choose the form best suited to him and his purposes. Vividly illustrated are the ways of overcoming shyness and fear which are inevitable in the initial stages of the Humor acquirement journey. In short, anyone who has decided to undertake this journey and has the determination to put in the sincere efforts required will find this book to be a very useful guide in reaching his destination; the person is sure to gain fabulous returns.

This book appears to address only the male readers as, in order to simplify reading, I have used male pronouns throughout the text. I would like to make it abundantly clear that this book addresses people of both sexes and all ages.

K. Sathyanarayana

Acknowledgements

I gratefully acknowledge the help rendered by the following by kindly permitting a reprint of previously published material:

- Alyssa Jackson for *Humor at Work*, by Esther Blumenfeld and Lynne Alpern, Peachtree Publishers.
- Clyde Fehlman for *Laughing 9 to 5*, Steelhead Press.
- Doubleday, a division of Random House Inc., for *10,000 Jokes, Toasts, & Stories*, edited by Lewis and Faye Copeland.
- Pat Williams for *Winning with One-liners*, Health Communications Inc.
- Raymond A. Moody, Jr., for *Laugh After Laugh*, Headwaters Press.
- Wendy Yoder for *The Speaker's Quote Book*, by Roy B. Zuck, Kregel Publications.

I am grateful to Sanjay Kirloskar for writing the Foreword to this book, and more importantly, for having been my role model with the "Armor of Humor." I am indebted to B.H. Agalgatti, who has been a source of continuous inspiration to me. My nephew, Ramki, put in untiring efforts to make a large number of reference books available to me. Mohan Kulkarni, Srinivas Vaidya and Satish Koushik, among others, have helped me by sharing their personal anecdotes. K.V. Gautam has done a splendid job in providing the appropriate cartoons that add to the appeal of the book.

Leela Kirloskar, Neha Kohli and others at Sage Publications have done a great job in correcting and improving my manuscript, and in bringing out the book in this form.

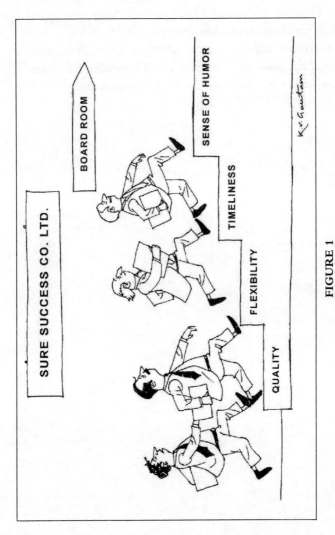

FIGURE 1
Humor: Stepping Stone for Success

Chapter 1

Humor: Mankind's Marvel!

"Humor is laughing at what you haven't got, when you ought to have it!"

—Langston Hughes

☺ *I would like to begin by quoting an incident which occurred when I was studying in high school; our headmaster asked our class a simple question: "Who is more powerful: the sun or the moon?"*

I guessed the answer immediately but thought it prudent to allow my classmates to give their answers first. But the class was silent even after a couple of minutes. The headmaster wondered why no one could answer such a simple question. My pride was hurt and I therefore boldly stood up and answered: "The moon is obviously more powerful."

I was asked to explain the logic behind my answer. With total confidence I said: "It's very clear that the moon is stronger; the sun gives us light when we already have light during the day. But the moon gives us light when it is dark, so the moon is clearly the more powerful."

All my classmates silently endorsed my logic, but the headmaster did not look satisfied. He laughed at me and said I was foolish to think that the daylight would continue to be there even when the sun wasn't. I immediately realized my mistake of taking daylight for granted.

As I grew older I realized that most of us take many more things for granted. Our health, our ability to sleep, our ability to forget embarrassment and misfortunes and our ability to wonder. The same applies to our Sense of Humor—our ability to laugh and smile, our ability to enjoy ourselves when tickled. Can we think of a world in which Humor has been totally banished? If we are forbidden to smile, laugh, enjoy, tease, taunt, crack jokes or play silly games, how can we live healthily? Let's take the case of our country: our people suffer from poverty, starvation, diseases, flood, drought, corrupt politicians and bureaucrats, and so on. But when we read something humorous in the newspapers or magazines, written by famous humorists, most of us feel compensated. This clearly proves that Humor can help us maintain our inner strength in the midst of outer turmoil.

Here are some examples of popular Humor by two of our famous humorists.

☺ *"The Indian police is to be awarded the prize for being the best police force in the world. Do you know why? They have knowledge about felonies and villainies even before they are carried out!"* —Jaspal Bhatti

☺ *"Do you know which is our national sport? Hockey? Cricket? Tennis? You're wrong in all these guesses. Our National Sport is 'Copying'! From fashion to films, from singing to sports, from scientific research to medicinal formulations, we Indians are super-specialists in imitating."* —Jaspal Bhatti

☺ *A cartoon in* The Times of India *under the heading, "You Said It", shows a scene at a municipal hospital. A patient waiting in line has finally reached the doctor and says: "Well, doctor, I was severely injured in an accident, but I am OK now! My wounds healed while I waited in the queue to get here!"* —R.K. Laxman

☺ *Another similar cartoon shows two policemen standing at one end of a street under a "NO-ENTRY" board; they are engaged in a dialogue. One says: "This is an ideal way, I think, to control traffic—we've put up a similar sign at the other end too!"* —R.K. Laxman

Defining Humor

It is not an easy task to precisely explain what Humor is. Dictionary meanings are either incomplete, inadequate, or vague. Humor is a complex subject for academic analysis; there are so many variations, contradictions, and inconsistencies in the parameters of Humor. Perhaps one can understand Humor more easily if the six levels in which Sense of Humor is displayed are explained. (These levels are based on the definitions of Raymond A. Moody, Jr., M.D., in his book, *Laugh After Laugh: The Healing Power of Humor*.)

First Level	*You laugh at a joke or funny story, only if and when, others laugh.*
Second Level	*You laugh at a joke or funny story, on your own, whether others laugh or not.*
Third Level	*You have a good collection of amusing jokes; you are experienced in telling them from your memory to others, to entertain them and make them laugh.*
Fourth Level	*In addition to the third level qualities, you have a certain degree of creativity which you use to make your own jokes, humorous stories, quips, etc.*
Fifth Level	*You can laugh at yourself in the presence of others; if others make fun of you, you can join their laughter. You don't lose your temper too quickly on such occasions.*
Sixth Level	*You do not take yourself too seriously. You can see any situation with some detachment, with an uncommon larger perspective. You are not upset by failures and can laugh and think positively even in a crisis. You can identify, realize, and respect reality, without getting emotionally involved. Your creed is to enjoy yourself in every situation.*

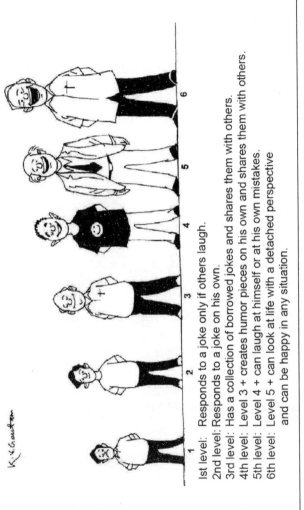

K. V. Gautam

1st level: Responds to a joke only if others laugh.
2nd level: Responds to a joke on his own.
3rd level: Has a collection of borrowed jokes and shares them with others.
4th level: Level 3 + creates humor pieces on his own and shares them with others.
5th level: Level 4 + can laugh at himself or at his own mistakes.
6th level: Level 5 + can look at life with a detached perspective
and can be happy in any situation.

FIGURE 2
The Six Levels of Humor

Humor touches every walk of life and every stratum of society. It takes on many forms: cartoons, animated stories, jokes, funny stories, one-liners, quotes, quips, proverbs, anecdotes, pranks, etc. As examples, read the following jokes.

> ☺ *I was once the chief guest at the local social club for its annual day function. When I rose to speak, the background noise also became too much. I complained to the president: "It's so noisy in here, that I can hardly hear myself speak." "Never mind," the president reassured me, "you didn't miss too much!"*

> ☺ *I signed up for an exercise class and the instructor asked us to come wearing tennis shoes and a loose-fitting dress. I went up to him and shared my grievance: "If I had any loose-fitting clothing, I wouldn't have signed up in the first place!"*

> ☺ *Patient: "Doctor, the medicine you prescribed was wonderful, the pain in my leg is gone. But I'm afraid that it makes me walk sideways."*
> *Doctor: "Well, I did warn you that there will be some side effects, didn't I?"*

When you read these three jokes, the first one amuses you slightly and makes you smile; the second one makes you laugh; and the last one brings forth a belly laugh.

Humor and Laughter

Even though Humor creates laughter quite frequently, laughter is not the test for Humor. Many forms and degrees of Humor can amuse and entertain, but they do not always make a person laugh. In the majority of cases, however, Humor does trigger laughter; and laughter, in turn, can occur in a number of patterns and degrees: chuckling, chortling, giggling, tittering, sniggering, guffawing, belly laughs, howling, hooting, roaring, cackling, and bellowing. What makes people laugh is widely varying; how people laugh differs from person to person. But everyone looks forward to a good laugh. Laughter enables you to accept failures and setbacks boldly, it imparts the strength and character to try again and again. Laughter helps you to enjoy life and it has been established that laughter can make us happy. There have been several examples where laughter has cured diseases which could not be cured by modern medicine.

Humor is very handy, subtle, and has multiple aspects. You may think of using it to achieve one purpose and be surprised to see it manifesting itself in several payoffs. It brings affinity, bridges dissimilarities, eases sharpness in censures, alleviates anxiety, mitigates nervousness, minimizes stress, softens suspense and confers a host of other ancillary advantages. Humor, therefore, is truly mankind's marvel. Both Humor and laughter can grant a person the correct perspective to look at life positively in all circumstances. Here are few examples.

Example 1

☺ *A well-known speaker met with a number of unexpected problems right at the beginning of his speech: his notes flew off from the lectern; the microphone attached to his necktie became loose and dropped down with a thud; and he had an attack of an unduly large number of loud and nasty sneezes.*

When he appeared to have recovered from all of these mishaps and was about to begin the speech, there was a shrill squawking noise sent forth by the audio system. The speaker, however, didn't look perturbed; he looked at the audience with a contented expression and said, "How do you like my performance so far?" The whole crowd applauded the speaker in appreciation of the fact that he looked totally confident. That one remark by the speaker had transformed him from a loser into a winner.

Example 2

☺ *Mahatma Gandhi was scheduled to address the citizens of Mysore at the Maharaja's College campus to enlist their active support for the Sarvodaya Movement. Even though Gandhiji was well known for his strict punctuality, on that day he had been held up at his earlier halt and his arrival at Mysore had therefore been delayed by about an hour. The people who had gathered and were eagerly awaiting the arrival of the chief guest grew somewhat restless. Some youths drew a picture of Gandhiji on a large sheet of paper and made that into a kite. When the kite rose high in the air, all the people came out to watch it. Gandhiji's car reached the venue at that moment. To attract the attention of the crowd to the program on hand, Gandhiji held the microphone in his hand and asked: "Dear friends, when the real Gandhi in flesh and blood is standing in front of you, why are you engaging yourselves in looking at a mere sketch of that man?" Immediately the whole crowd made its way to the auditorium.* (You will observe how Gandhiji, who was very hard pressed for time, used Humor to strike a quick rapport with the audience and sought their cooperation for commencing his talk without further delay.)

Example 3

☺ *When Gandhiji was engaged in "Sathyagraha" (Non-cooperation Movement) in South Africa, the government sent a civil court judge along with the police to arrest him at midnight. The judge knocked on Gandhiji's door and declared their intentions. Gandhiji welcomed the judge with a broad smile and said, "Till now juniors from the police department used to come to arrest me. But today, it appears that I've been promoted by your government. A civil judge coming to arrest me means a real promotion to me! Won't you congratulate me?"*

Humor is an important and essential resource when you negotiate or deal with an adversary. It helps you to relax. Proper use of Humor does not call for ignoring your problems; instead, it stimulates your creativity and enables you to come up with innovative answers to the problems at hand. See the following examples.

Example 1

☺ *In 1960, the two erstwhile superpowers of this world, the US and the Soviet Union, were on the verge of starting the Third World War. Fortunately, sanity prevailed on both sides and the world was saved from a catastrophe. What happened was that the Soviet Union installed a number of powerful long range missiles on Cuban soil and the US government, not pleased with this Soviet move, objected strongly. The US President gave an ultimatum to the Soviet Union, that if the missiles were not removed within the time period set by the US, the Soviet Union should prepare itself for a full-fledged war with the US and its allies. The Soviet leaders were not ready for any war and they immediately sent their diplomats to negotiate with the US Government.*

The negotiators of both camps found that there was enormous tension in the air at the meeting room. Someone suggested that it was necessary to reduce this tension and to achieve this purpose, each delegate should share a funny story or tell a joke. Everyone agreed. It was generally expected that the American delegates would be in the lead to take the stage. But it was a Russian who stood up first and asked the group: "Do you know that communism is quite different from capitalism? Do you know the difference?" "In capitalism," he went on, "Man exploits man; but in communism, it's exactly the other way around!" This had the whole group belly laughing. All the tension had disappeared and when the members resumed official discussions, there was a sense of mutual appreciation among them.

Next time when you want to rebuke someone for his shoddy work, try out this experiment. Instead of your customary tirade to lambast the defaulter, give a mild admonition cloaked with some exhortation. You'll see that your point is better understood by that person. When you happen to fly into a rage while criticizing, you're causing your listeners to reciprocate to your wild temper. He or she ceases to listen to you and will focus in finding out your faults and failures. Both of you are losers and chances of improvement are very dim. Instead, if you say to the person: "It seems that both of us have a little problem," with a smiling face and explain how to resolve the issue, you can expect a much more useful and positive response. Your listener is not insulted and is, therefore, more receptive to your demands for improvement. Consider the following examples.

Example 1

☺ The boxer swiped the air furiously but could not hit his opponent.

"How am I doing?" he asked his coach at the end of the round.

"Well, if you keep this up", replied the coach, "he might feel the draught and catch a cold!"

Example 2

☺ My daughter's husband bought an exercise machine to help him shed a few kilos. He set it up in the basement, but didn't use it much and so moved it to the bedroom. It gathered dust there too, so he put it in the living room. But the machine was seldom used. One day my daughter remarked:

"You're right, Pranav; you do get more exercise now. Every time you close the drapes, you have to walk around the machine!"

Example 3

☺ The Boss called Hari after the annual performance appraisal; Hari was very buoyant when he sat before the Boss. The latter said, "Hari, I have decided to offer you a salary rise; what do you say?"

Hari: "Sir, thank you very much; from when would the rise become effective?"

Boss: "Oh, that would be as soon as you become really effective!"

Example 4

☺ Boss: *"Shyam, I want to congratulate you."*
Shyam: *"Why sir?"*
Boss: *"On your expertise in concentrating all your initiative,
imagination, and know-how into your expense account!"*

The most important step in any problem-solving situation
is to free yourself from excessive seriousness with which
you view the problem. Just as you would not be able to see
a picture if it is held too close to your eyes, unwarranted
seriousness dries up your creative juices and makes you tense
and worked up. If you are able to relax when you face a
problem, your subconscious mind can take over and enable
you to think up imaginative solutions to the problem. It is
not easy to have a problem on hand and relax. This is exactly
when Humor can be helpful. It provides the proper
perspective to look at things, with a certain degree of detach-
ment. Too many systems, procedures, rules, and regulations
check originality, suppress the imagination, and smother
inventiveness. The most conducive environment for
problem solving is created by light-heartedness, laughter,
and Humor. Take a look at the following instances where
this has worked.

Example 1

☺ *Creative problem solving has been resorted to by many and
Walt Disney deserves a special mention here because of
his ultra-original ideas. The scheduled day of inaugurating
Disneyland was close at hand, but the landscaping work of*

the park was still far from completion. Moreover, as Disney was facing a severe fund crisis he could not give any push to the pending work. It was then that Disney thought of an amazing solution to the landscaping problems. Disney observed that all the decorative plants in the park had been labeled in Latin. He called his gardener and asked him to also get the Latin names of all the weeds in the park and label them. The problem was thus solved and the landscaping of the park was "completed" with all the weeds bearing Latin labels.

Example 2

☺ A young school girl who had not secured good grades in her exams at school felt that she would be severely reprimanded at home about this. Therefore, when she reached home that day, she confided to her mother that she was pregnant. Naturally, the family members were shocked. The girl waited till the emotions in the house had cooled down before declaring "You need not worry; I'm not pregnant. All of you can now cheer up; but I got very poor grades at school. Now I hope you'll excuse me for that."

Example 3

☺ Mr Gupta fell sick and was bedridden. Mrs Gupta took her husband to the doctor. The doctor, who was quite close to the Guptas, examined the patient and gave some pills to the lady saying: "These are some sleeping pills."

The lady interrupted the doctor and asked: "When do I give them to him, doctor?"

> *"No, you don't give them to him", said the doctor, "You will take them, one every six hours!"*

Example 4

☺ *An Albanian visited the US with the intention of buying some production machinery. The president of the US company from whom the Albanian was to buy the machinery was giving his guest a factory tour. When the lunch whistle blew, all the workers went out for lunch and when the whistle blew a second time, all the workers rushed in. The guest was so impressed, that instead of buying the machine, he ordered the whistle!*

Successful people and companies employ Humor to create a lively outlook. For example, our newspapers include cartoons and comics to cheer us up and to prevent us from becoming unduly depressed by the news we read about our politicians, police, and public. Our magazines carry Humor pages for the same purpose. Humor helps you to induce laughter in any situation. For example, try to magnify the problem you currently have by asking yourself:

"Is it going to kill me?"
"Will it cause an earthquake?"
"Will it cause a tsunami?"
"Will it last for five years?"
"Will I think of it after five years from now?"

Perhaps you will discover that you will laugh at it after five years. Humor will prompt you to laugh at it right now, instead of five years later.

Edison

☺ *By the age of 12, Thomas Edison had a job on the Grand Trunk Railway selling newspapers to passengers as the train traveled between Port Huron and Detroit. Being highly enterprising, Edison was soon publishing his own newspaper,* The Weekly Herald, *from the baggage car of the train, based on the new stories gleamed from telegraph offices along the route. Edison used the income from this enterprise to fund his chemistry experiments.*

One day, arriving at the station just as the train was leaving, Edison jumped on to the train from the platform and just about managed to catch the last step. He was, however, unable to pull himself up. Luckily, a conductor came to his rescue and pulled him aboard. However, as the conductor happened to pull Edison by the ear, Edison felt something snap in his head. From that day Edison developed progressive deafness. Edison did not feel bad about his disability. Instead, he was sometimes happy that the silence afforded him the ability to concentrate while others were busy gossiping. Edison was richly rewarded for his new perspective. He became the first scientist to record sound. Can you believe it? A deaf man succeeding in recording sound!

Humor: Tolerance

When things are beyond your control, Humor tells you to become a graceful willow, instead of standing erect like the tall silver oak tree. When the wind blows, the willow swings, sways, and swerves, to stand up again. The silver oak tree which rigidly bristles upright is most likely to snap and crash. See the following examples.

FIGURE 3
The Willow and the Oak Tree

Example 1

☺ *During the Second World War, Hitler's modernized German air force bombarded Great Britain ruining a number of British cities and towns. Even in the face of such adversity, the British people displayed a rare Sense of Humor; some of the shopkeepers who had lost their roofs, erected bold signboards: saying "We're more open for business!"*

Example 2

☺ *Long before he became a candidate for the presidency, Adlai Stevenson owned a grand house near Lake Forest, Illinois. Shortly after he and his family moved in, the house was destroyed by a fire. While Stevenson watched his house go up in flames, a piece of smoldering wood landed near his feet. He picked the wood up and used it to light his cigarette. Then he turned to the fire officer and said: "At least I'm still getting some use out of the house!"*

Humor Reframes Ideas

A creative mind can make the most harsh conditions acceptable by adding a humorous note. Queueing and waiting are unavoidable wherever you go. Car makers provide gadgets so that you can listen to the radio or your favorite music to reduce the boredom while waiting in line for the traffic signal to change. Some banks provide piano music to customers awaiting their turn. Airports and large railway stations telecast news, serials/soaps, and movies on television screens placed at convenient points to entertain the passengers waiting to board.

Example 1

> ☺ *Two stone-cutters were engaged at a site where a church was to be built. One of them felt the urge to smoke and when he was about to light the cigarette, the other said to him, "Hey, do you have the permission of the bishop, to smoke here?"*
>
> *The first man went to the bishop and asked, "Father, can I smoke while I'm working?"*
>
> *The bishop rejected the request and so the man returned disappointed. His companion asked him as to what happened and assured him the he would get the bishop's approval within a minute. So saying, he went to the bishop and came back laughing and said to his colleague, "The Father has approved; let's enjoy!"*
>
> *While smoking, the first stone-cutter was curious to learn the secret of his colleague's achievement. Pat came the reply: "You didn't know how to ask. I asked the bishop, whether working was alright while smoking; he gladly approved it!"*

The manner in which a request, a suggestion, a proposal, or an offer is made, often decides the receiver's response. Properly framed words, their articulation, the emphasis given, etc., are very important in order to get a favorable reception. Humor helps to dress up bad news; it causes less embarrassment when you have to relate your failures.

Example 2

> ☺ *Emperor Akbar, dreamt a funny dream one night. Next morning he called upon a great astrologer, explained his dream, and asked about its significance. The astrologer*

referred to his ancient books, made some calculations using all his fingers, went around the emperor's bedroom three times along with the emperor, and announced the significance: "All the relatives of the emperor will die during his lifetime."

Akbar became terribly angry upon hearing this and had the astrologer imprisoned. He then sent for Birbal, the great humorist, and when Birbal came, sought his views about the punishment to be meted out to the poor astrologer. Birbal listened to the detailed account of the incident which had made Akbar angry and then said: "Huzur, the dream you had last night is very auspicious. It says that among all the members of your family, you will live the longest." Akbar was very happy to hear this and he rewarded Birbal profusely. Later, when Akbar was in a merry mood, Birbal pleaded that mercy be shown to the astrologer whose prediction, though correct, was clothed in unwelcome words.

Example 3

☺ American Airlines had named their overnight flights as "Red-Eye Flights" and were suffering heavy losses because of them. Somehow they had failed to attract passengers and hence the flights were near empty. In a spirited drive to im-prove the conditions, the airlines changed the name of these flights to "Midnight Special." Free music videos and free champagne were provided making Midnight Special a thoroughly enjoyable and fun flight. These steps improved occupancy by more than 70 percent and the flights became quite profitable.

Humor Defuses Criticism and Hostility

Humor is not beating around the proverbial bush; many business situations call for candor. For example, when your people are not delegating enough or when they fail to deliver the desired quality/quantity; or when they do not effectively communicate, they have to be cautioned about these shortfalls. But this process should not dampen their commitment nor damage their goodwill. Humor can be a great help in such situations. Some examples of how criticism can be soft and how hostility can be defused are given below.

☺ *US President, John F. Kennedy appointed his brother, Robert Kennedy to be the Federal Attorney General. This step attracted widespread criticism and was labeled as misplaced favoritism. One news reporter questioned the President in an interview on whether his decision was the correct choice. The President's answer was a loaded one: "What's wrong with giving Robert an opportunity to gain some judicial experience as attorney general, before he starts his law practice!"*

☺ *Charles Steinmetz, the famous engineer, was once called out of retirement by General Electric Company to help them locate a problem in an intricate system of complex machines. Having spent some time tinkering with and testing various parts of the system, Steinmetz finally placed a chalk mark "X" on a small component in one machine. GE's engineers promptly examined the component and were amazed to find the defect in the precise location of Steinmetz's mark.*

Some days later GE received an invoice for $10,000 from the wily engineer. The company protested that it was incredulous and challenged Steinmetz to itemise it. Steinmetz did it readily: "Making one chalk mark–$1, knowing where to put it–$9,999!"

☺ Wife : *"You are becoming more and more cruel towards me. You've totally forgotten my birthday. Do I need anymore evidence that you have stopped loving me?"*

   Husband : *"Darling, it is not like that. How can you expect me to remember your birthday when you have remained exactly as beautiful as you were a year ago!"*

☺ *When Ronald Reagan was campaigning for getting reelected as US President, Walter Mondale, his rival, attacked Reagan's candidature on the grounds that the latter was too old for the post of President. In the early days of the campaign, it looked as though Reagan would lose to Mondale, but Reagan's deputies worked overnight over their election strategy. In his next speech, Reagan declared: "I want you to know, that I will not make age an issue in this campaign. I am not going to exploit, for political purposes, my opponent's youth and inexperience."*

This humorous approach made everyone laugh. Even Mondale laughed. This became the turning point in the election and led to Reagan's victory.

☺ *In the Lincoln-Douglas debates, Stephen A. Douglas accused Lincoln of being two-faced. "I leave it to you, my friends," Lincoln retorted turning towards the audience, "If I had two faces, would I be wearing this one?"*

Humor and Tension/ Embarrassments

As explained earlier, Humor is a tool with multiple aspects and it has variety of applications. But in today's hectic world, its contribution in minimizing tension can be considered as the most beneficial. A little demo and few examples can explain how this takes place.

Demo

Push out both your hands in front of you. Form a fist with your left hand and hold your left wrist with your right hand, clamping it firmly. Now loosen your left fist. You'll observe that your right hand also automatically loses its grip. Humor works in exactly the same way. When you're relaxed your Humor invites the other person to also relax. Both of you will now be more at ease, more amenable, gracious, responsive, and transparent.

Example 1

☺ *In a courtroom, two opposing lawyers are engaged in a verbal duel. In the heat of the moment, one of them says to the other: "You're a fool of the first degree!"*

The other shouts a rejoinder: "You're an idiot of the last degree!"

The judge who wanted to bring the situation under control, struck the gavel saying in a loud voice. "You both are forgetting that I'm here!"

Example 2

☺ *The local bank was granting housing loans. One interested customer said: "Sir, I have mortgaged my property with you. I have assigned my insurance policy in your favor. I have arranged two guarantors also. Thank God! You are not asking me to mortgage my wife!"*

The processing clerk calmly replied without any hesitation or embarrassment: "No sir, we take only assets, not liabilities!"

Example 3

☺ *President Abraham Lincoln was once on a tour of the front-lines during the Civil War. The Union Army captain, Oliver Wendell Holmes, was assigned to escort the President. Pointing to a distant hill, Holmes told the President that it was occupied by rebel forces. Lincoln stood up to get a better look and was greeted by a barrage of gunfire. The President had unknowingly done a foolish thing by exposing himself to a serious danger. Without thinking, Holmes screamed: "Get down, you fool!"*

The President quickly obeyed. When they moved to safer quarters, Holmes felt highly embarrassed that he had called the President a fool. Lincoln, as he was about to leave, thanked Holmes for the tour and said: "I'm glad to see you know how to talk to a civilian."

This remark made it clear to Holmes that what he had done was absolutely correct and that the President was happy with the officer's dedication to duty. Lincoln's greatness is evidenced in the Humor he employed to make Holmes feel at ease and to convince him that he did not carry any ill will towards him.

Humor and Stress

All animals as well as human beings are provided by nature with a physiological system, which comes into action whenever any danger is perceived. Danger triggers a "Fight or Flight" syndrome, forces adrenalin into the body, and sets off a host of reactions which stimulate peak level body activities. Peak level activity lasts for a short duration, after which the body is exhausted. Ordinarily, an individual may not encounter any such danger to his/her life, yet the responses of an individual's body even to a little danger could be the same as when life is under threat.

Some stress is essential for progress. Positive stress is stimulating and helps a person to succeed. It is the stepping stone to efficiency and effectiveness. On the other hand, if the intensity of stress, its duration, or its frequency becomes excessive, then stress is more likely to rush a person into life-saving mode with all its exhaustion and not-so-desirable side effects. Humor can protect you from such an ordeal. Try this experiment to understand the dynamics involved.

When you are in an extremely embarrassing situation next time, sit tightly and catch hold of the arms of your chair; tighten all the muscles of your body and hold your breath. Now try to maintain the same body stiffness, but breathe out and smile from ear to ear. You'll observe that when you smile broadly, the stiffness of the body is lost. You are compelled to relax. You will also feel a sense of relief.

What has happened? Your smile has banished stress and tension. Laughter, which is an enlarged version of a smile, is even more effective. Remember to fight stress with Humor to enjoy life and be successful. Let's look at some examples of Humor and stress.

Example 1

☺ *Ravi Yadav, Professor of Economics, was telling Dr Sharmila Shah who happened to be a psychologist, "I'm a walking economy."*

Dr Shah: "How so?"

Professor Yadav: "My hairline is in recession, my paunch line is a victim of inflation; both these together are putting me into a depression!"

Example 2

☺ *A Mumbai motorist was driving through the sugarcane belt of southern Maharashtra. While driving on NH–4 near Karad, he hit and killed a calf. The motorist offered the owner of the calf compensation for his loss. The motorist asked the farmer: "How much was your calf worth?"*

The farmer thought for a long time and consulted his friends who had gathered at the scene of the accident. "The calf was worth Rs 1,000 today," said the farmer, "But it would have been worth Rs 6,000 in six years!"

The motorist wrote out a cheque for Rs 6,000, post-dated six years from that day!

Example 3

☺ *Franklin Delano Roosevelt, popularly known as FDR, former President of USA, was once asked how he managed to retain his composure in the face of the difficulties which plagued his presidency, for example, the Great Depression, World War II, etc. Roosevelt who, when he was young, had contracted polio and was almost on his death-bed because of* this malady, had a ready reply: "If you spent two years in bed trying to wiggle your big toe," he remarked, "after that everything would seem easy!"

Example 4

☺ Hedley Verity, the wily Yorkshire spin bowler, was always a nightmare for the batsmen of the opposing team; his skill and guile made it extremely difficult for them to hit his balls. But once a South African batsman was in a punishing mood; he scored off Verity two sixes and three fours in one murderous over, leaving Verity shocked and bruised. A colleague of Verity tried to cheer him up by saying, "Cheer up Hedley! You have posed that bugger a big puzzle."

"What puzzle?" asked the hapless Verity. "What do you mean?"

"Can't you see? Poor chap! He is confused whether to hit you for a four or a six!"

Example 5

☺ The well-known tennis player Illie Nastasse once lost his American Express credit card. But he was not very quick in reporting his loss to the authorities. His argument was that the finder of the card would not be able to match his wife in spending and so he had reason to be happy about the loss of the card.

Example 6

☺ Two Soviet youths managed to flee their country to the US and led happy lives as fugitives in the host country for a few

*years. Gradually, however, they became homesick and decided
to return to their homeland. As they were not very sure that
they would not be sent to the Siberian concentration camps
by the government/authorities for their none too patriotic
conduct, they agreed to be cautious. Instead of both returning
together they decided that only one would go back first and
would inform the other of the conditions over there. They
tossed a coin to decide which of the two should go back first.
The guy who was to go back first said, "If I find the situation
agreeable, I will use black ink and if otherwise I will use red
ink. The colour of the ink used will describe the conditions
more eloquently, than the words used."*

*A few months passed since the departure of the youth who
had left for his homeland but there was no communication
from him to the guy in the US who was anxiously awaiting
his feedback. At long last he received a letter, which had aged
excessively during its transit, written in black ink, "I'm very
happy to say that things are very nice here. Please come back
immediately. I'm fully okay; the only problem I'm having, is
that I could not get red ink even though I tried very hard!"*

Humor and Communication

Surveys show that a vast majority of people spend a major
portion of their waking time in communications-related
activities. This may involve talking with someone directly
or over the phone, writing to someone, or thinking about
how to communicate. The main goal of almost all communication is to influence the other person or persons to think,
do, or behave in the ways the communicator wants.

The most beneficial way of strengthening communication skills is to judiciously use appropriate Humor. Humor generates respect, grabs the listener's attention, and helps an audience remember the message. It defuses the attack of your opponents, motivates and inspires listeners into action, and thereby helps getting results. Whatever may be the type of communication—oral or written, one-to-one or one-to-a-group, direct or through media—Humor can be a powerful ally when three factors, namely, the lead-in, relevance, and appropriateness are taken care of. Consider the examples below.

Example 1

☺ *Bob Murphey, the famous humorist, had a funny habit. As soon as he entered the hall in which his speech had been arranged, he would look out for the Exits. He was not afraid of a fire breakout, as he had served as a voluntary fireman and therefore never feared fire. He was also not nervous of a terrorist attack; he was confident that the law and order authorities and the security staff of the five-star hotel would have taken adequate precautions. All that he feared were the guys who would catch hold of him and insist on telling him jokes in their own insipid style.*

Example 2

☺ *In 1962, the King of Greece came to India on a state visit. Welcoming him, President Sarvapalli Radhakrishnan said: "Your Majesty, You're the first King of Greece to come here as our guest; Alexander came uninvited!"*

Example 3

☺ *A husband and wife entered into an argument which soon became very heated as both wanted to win. The husband proposed: "Let's not lose our cool, darling ... I suggest we be logical and put forth our views peacefully."*

"Not at all," retorted the wife, "Whenever I talk with you logically and peacefully, you always manage to win!"

Example 4

☺ *Mark Twain opened one of his speeches, with the following words: "I'm different from George Washington. I have a higher standard of principle. Washington couldn't tell a lie. I can lie, but I won't!"*

All these examples illustrate how powerful Humor can be. Humor is not always the dramatic quotable line that makes the morning paper and alters history. A good Sense of Humor is mostly an attitude. It's a commonsense way of looking at yourself and the world around you. Your communication is not merely for the purpose of getting laughs or even applause. It is there to make a point, to influence the receiver in a way you want. Humor is a tool in your hand to enable you to achieve it. Most of us wrongly believe that Humor is the attribute possessed only by some gifted persons like Mark Twain, Johny Walker, Bob Hope, Danny Kaye, R.K. Laxman and the like. It is true that everyone who picks up a brush cannot become a Ravi Verma or Picasso; similarly, you may not become a world famous humorist, comedian, or comic writer. It is not necessary either. But you should note that a Sense of Humor is a gift which everyone possesses; anyone who has laughed has proved beyond doubt that he has a Sense of Humor. All that is required is to nurture it and strengthen it by conscious effort regularly.

Conclusion

The rewards that Humor can confer on us are many. Humor fills life with fun. It makes communicating interesting and effective. Humor enables you to accept the harsh and unpleasant truths of life. Humor enables you to face problems and resolve them and provides an agreeable way to vent irritations and dissatisfaction. It moderates aggressive behavior and makes you team better with the group. It does not pose problems of obesity. It does not cost money. It improves physical and mental health. Humor has proved to succeed where other approaches have not worked. Humor makes you look humane and real.

Chapter 2

Smile Please, We're at Work!

*"We set three objectives of NATD (North American Tool and Die).
First, we planned to grow the company profitably. Second, to share
the wealth with employees. And third, and equally critical, it was
important to have fun—not just the two owners, but all our employees.
And this is the key—to have fun!"*

—Tom Melohn

The orthodox view is that it is foolish to have Humor at
the workplace. Many managers believe that work and fun
don't go together, because they think fun to be nothing
short of escape from work. They also say that work is a
grave task; grimness, grittiness, sustained vigilance, anxious
and scowling faces are the essential features of a well
managed workplace. If any worker happens to be laughing
or is caught displaying a fun loving attitude, it is concluded
that he is insincere, inferior, and hence, unfit.

Even today, a number of organizations stick to this
outmoded view. They believe that employees are contracted
for the sole purpose of putting in work and as fun at the
workplace leads to poor output, it should be banned totally.

One additional reason for many people sticking to this
belief could lie in their past: in childhood recollections of
their parents despising their daily work. Perhaps these parents
shuddered while going about their jobs in the fields, or in
shops. As a result, their children started believing that work
meant pure and total slaving, and that the workplace was
an annoying and troublesome but inescapable compulsion
of life, just like illness and disease. This traditional perception
inculcated in young minds may be the root of such
jaundiced thinking that work and play are antonyms.

The view just discussed is a fallacy and not the truth. To
ascertain for yourself whether or not work and play can go
together, carry out this simple experiment. On one of your

very busy days, take a short break from your work, listen to a scintillating song or read a comical story, and then resume working. Check whether you feel pleasantly stimulated; you'll certainly feel re-energized. This proves that when you enjoy your work, you will become more effective, not less!

You can examine this issue from another angle. Suppose your boss gives you the job of carrying, daily, a 10 kg sack from Point A to Point B, 10 km away, and after delivering it at Point B, carrying another 10 kg sack from Point B to Point A. During the course of your work, you will observe that every additional hour makes the sack more heavy and that you are left totally exhausted at the end of the day. Your body aches and you feel totally drained—both physically and mentally. You are now worried about whether you would be able to resume work the next day.

Imagine, now, that instead of carrying out your job in one go you rest for short periods, every hour; you keep the sack down during the rest period and stretch your limbs. You even forget the sack while resting. After the break, you pick up the sack and resume work. You will now find that the sack is in no way heavier than when you lifted it for the first time. At the end of the day you'll be free from the unbearable body ache and discover your mental faculties to be in much better shape too. You will not dread going to work the next day. The following examples attribute to the success of Humor at the workplace.

Humor and Common Sense

☺ *The other day, I met the Managing Director (MD) of a very reputed Indian engineering company, which once was an*

*also ran, as far as its bottom line was concerned. The MD
had taken over the reins of the company at a very young
age and was somewhat unconventional in his approach
to managing the affairs of the company. He took time to
make himself familiar with the company's operations and
applied his methods for improvement gradually. Today, this
company is the largest exporter of the products it manufactures
and has also been making very good profits regularly; its
shares are blue chips on the stock exchanges. When I asked
the MD the secret of his success, he replied, "Common Sense!"
He added that he practices Humor to create a positive
atmosphere all round and spices up his memos, telephone
talks, presentations, and criticisms with Humor.*

Growing a Business

☺ *Paul Hawkins (Paul Hawken), the American entrepreneur
and author of the 1983 best-seller,* Growing a Business,
*has said: "If you and your employees, customers and vendors
don't have a good time, if the laughter has died out, you're
in the wrong Business!"*

Three Real Things!

☺ *John F. Kennedy, former US President, once quoted, an old
Arab saying: "There are three things which are real: God,
human folly, and laughter. The first two are beyond
comprehension. So, we must do, what we can do with the
third!"*

Turnaround Secret!

☺ Before Lee Iacocca was appointed the Chief Executive Officer (CEO) of Chrysler Motors, the company was on the verge of closing down because of the heavy losses it was incurring, year after year. Iacocca firmly believed that the company could be turned around by enlisting the collaboration and involvement of all the employees. During his very first week at Chrysler, Iacocca started meeting all the plant managers one by one, at their respective workplaces. He got himself introduced to each manager and chatted with them for a few minutes, over soft drinks and cookies. Iacocca would ask the manager what he thought the management should do to improve matters. Iacocca continued with such meetings regularly and has acknowledged that 80 percent of the plans he implemented to eventually turn the company around were contributed by the plant managers during such meetings. Iacocca knew very well that a certain degree of cosiness and informality were essential to foster innovativeness and to dispel the fear factor associated with CEO-manager relationships.

Novel Interviewing!

☺ Nancy Hauge, director, Human Resources, at Sun Microsystems has stated, "Generally, in interviews, I mentally note down how long it takes the candidate to laugh, how long it takes him to find something funny or share his Sense of Humor. It is my experience that persons with a better Sense of Humor handle tough problems better, without getting cowed down."

Practical Humor!

> ☺ *The personnel manager of a mega company was interviewing applicants for filling a vacancy in their publicity division. One of the applicants claimed that he had rich experience as a writer of humorous scripts for TV programs. The human resource manager was keen to verify the truth in this claim so he asked the applicant to demonstrate his talent. Without any hesitation the fellow got up, opened the office door, leaned into the waiting room and in a loud and clear voice said, " Well, you guys, you can go home! The vacancy has just now been filled in!"*
>
> *Needless to say that he got the job.*

Humor breaks at the workplace achieve the same purpose of restoring your physical and psychic stamina. Humor enables you to gain respite from your work-related troubles and trepidations in order to relax and rejuvenate yourself. So, would it not be prudent to encourage your employees to display a Sense of Humor and to start learning how to enjoy their work?

Bob Ross, the author in his book *That's a good one!*, explains a very valid point when he discusses the two styles of people functioning: the formal and the informal. In the formal style, you tend to be shy, diffident, introverted, and very cautious. You are likely to avoid all embarrassing situations and dodge every risky idea. You abhor any change and are always for preserving current practices. You are averse to all new ideas and improvements. Your body is tense, your general appearance grim, your face more likely to wear a scowl, and your limbs set in a defensive stance.

The formal style was ushered in the 18th century and was popular until the middle of the 20th Century. In any enterprise, the main assets were money and machinery. People were thoroughly exploited by the owner who patronized the formal style. Employee participation was unheard of; all decisions were taken by the owner only. However, this style of functioning had its days numbered, as the second half of the 20th century saw sweeping changes in the whole economy, which heralded the informal style of functioning.

Lee Iacocca, the famous one-time CEO of Chrysler Corporation, served earlier at the Ford Motor Company. He had this to say about the then management at Ford: "In the prewar years there was no intelligent management at Ford. When I arrived at the end of the war, the company was a monolithic dictatorship...."

In the informal style, you are nearer to your natural self; free from tension and imagined fears. You are likely to be experimental and willing to take some risks. You are not afraid of failure. You look forward to giving and receiving new ideas. You're ready to accept yourself as you are, and do not hesitate to accept the people around you as they are. You indulge in being playful and having fun. Physically, you are at ease and your body is relaxed. You have a comfortable stance and are ready to smile. Your looks are likely to make the people around you relax and be candid.

The informal style of functioning respects all people; it promotes a broader outlook, encourages people to be innovative, fosters forthrightness, and permits playfulness. It is in this environment that the intuitive and innovative part of your mind becomes active. (While this style is ideal for the vast majority of work situations, there could be a few occasions when this is not appropriate. For example, when there is an emergency, the leader has to make on-the-spot decisions and muster strict obedience from his people.)

☺ *Henry Ford once invited a productivity consultant to assess the scope for improvement in his company. The consultant, in his report, stated, "The operations are generally satisfactory; but I have my own doubts about one employee, who has his office down the corridor. Whenever I saw him he was just sitting with his feet on his desk. He's certainly wasting company money."*

Henry Ford remarked, "That man once saved millions of dollars to the company. He used to plant his feet right where they're now!"

☺ *A young applicant for a job was asked, "Are you married?"*

"No," he replied, "but I know how to take orders, if that's what you mean!"

He was selected.

☺ *A teenage youth was considered by his parents to be good for nothing and this made the teenager more determined to get his first job during the summer vacation at the neighborhood bicycle shop. The owner of the shop asked the youth: "Do you have any experience in dealing with angry customers?"*

"I have not handled any angry customers so far," replied the youth, "but I've plenty of experience in handling angry parents!"

His ready wit won him the job.

☺ *My son was taking the written test during the selection of graduate trainees for a reputed engineering company in Maharashtra. One of the questions was: "Why is the word 'Psychic' spelt with a P?"*

My son didn't have the answer to this puzzler, but he was not happy to leave the question unanswered. He wrote, "It pcertainly does pseem psilly!"

☺ *Charles Kettering (1876–1958), the famous American electrical engineer and inventor was, in the early days of his career, supervising the erection of telephone poles in Ohio. A small group of men assisted him in this work. One day, during lunch hour, a beggar approached Kettering asking for some food. Kettering took a fancy to this man, led him to a nearby eatery, and ordered lunch for both of them. During the course of the meal, Kettering asked his guest whether he was interested in a job. The beggar was delighted and said he was ready to start work immediately.*

Kettering provided the fellow with the tackle and left the site in order to attend to some other job. When he returned after a few hours, he found his new employee digging a hole in the ground. It was not easy for the beggar to make good progress, for the ground was hard and he was not used to any hard work. The beggar perspired profusely; his back started aching, his limbs shook with the strain, his palms became blistered. Still, he continued digging. Kettering spoke encouragingly to the beggar and started digging a hole to demonstrate to the man how a good quality hole would look. Kettering's hole was perfectly circular, with straight smooth walls, and a flat bottom. Kettering explained these features to the beggar and remarked that he found it great fun to dig quality holes. The beggar was highly impressed by Kettering's feat and words; soon he started practicing digging quality holes and, in due course, became not only the best hole digger, but also the foreman of the gang. He expressed his gratitude to Kettering, and what he said was really significant: "You're the first person to tell me that work could be fun. If only someone had taught me this a few years ago, I never would have become a beggar!"

You can validate the essence of this narrative with your own experience. Try to recollect events in your life right from your childhood. Can you remember any moments of glory, when you performed outstandingly and stood out as best? It may be a brilliant performance in the mid-term class examination, or rendering a song in a singing competition, or a superb show at the college basketball match; what exactly your act was is not so important. But it should have been your peak performance, for which you had worked hard, made elaborate preparations, and took all necessary precautions to climax at the right moment. Now try to recapture the eagerness, anticipation and zeal you felt, while you prepared and performed. Did you enjoy the activity or did you find it boring and burdensome? Don't you agree that you excelled only because you found the activity exciting and enjoyable? Otherwise your performance would have been mediocre and you wouldn't have remembered it. It is this urge for self-fulfillment which leads you to excellence; a sense of plodding or slogging will take you away from excellence.

☺ *Margaret Thatcher, the Prime Minister of Britain from May 1979 to November 1990, who held the record of the longest uninterrupted tenure as British PM, used to share one of her experiences very often in her talks: "I had applied for a job in 1948 and was called for a personal interview. However I failed to get selected. Many years later, I succeeded in finding out why I had been rejected. The remarks written by the selectors on my application were: 'This woman is headstrong, obstinate, and dangerously self-opinionated!'"*

It is really funny that the same qualities made her the longest continuously serving Prime Minister of her country.

She was both admired and despised. Her radical economic policies reversed decades of decline and reinstated Britain as a major economic force.

☺ Igor Stravinsky, the famous Russian-born music composer, was once offered US$ 4,000 to compose the musical score for a film. Stravinsky felt that the offered amount was too meagre. The Hollywood producer's argument in favor of the amount was that it was the same sum they had paid to the earlier music composer. Stravinsky was undeterred: "Ah, but my predecessor had talent," he replied, "and I have not, which makes the work for me much more difficult!"

Both of them laughed heartily. The composer was asked to name his fees, and it was accepted by the producer without any further argument.

☺ The MD of diesel engine manufacturing company was in an important meeting with his vice presidents (VPs). A product line, introduced by the company earlier that year, had been a total failure. The VPs knew about it and so did the MD, who was ready to take responsibility for the failure of the new engine business. Before saying anything on the subject, the MD narrated the following story: "I saw the other day, a man parking his car where parking was prohibited. A police constable came on the scene and politely asked the man to remove his car from the No Parking zone. But the car owner paid no heed. The policeman warned the man that if the car was not immediately removed, he would levy a fine of Rs 200 on him. The car owner retorted by saying India was a free country and that he could park his car anywhere he wanted. Just then a second policeman arrived and ordered the immediate removal of the car. Seeing the reluctance of the car owner, the second policeman lifted his stick and gave the disobeying civilian's back a not-so-gentle *hit. Immediately the man got into his car silently and moved it out from there and into the parking area.*

The first policeman was curious to know why the man was obstinate with him. The car owner replied. "You didn't explain to me in the way he did!"

After narrating the above story, the MD continued, "My dear fellows, now that the marketplace has explained to us the true situation properly, we have learnt our lesson!" The MD did not make scapegoats of his deputies; instead he took stock of the failure and took the blame himself. This drew the VPs closer to the MD. They would never again fear failures and would henceforth be more enterprising in their work. They would work hard and smart, to make the failed project successful. All these because of the humorous way the MD saw the situation.

Till recently, very little research was carried out on Humor in general, and Humor in business in particular. This has been the case because the complexity of the subject, the innumerable varieties of Humor and the multitude of factors involved made any structured study, formidable. Yet all this while, the importance of Humor in all facets of human endeavor has been rapidly mounting. So a number of researchers, notably in America and Europe, have been accepting this challenge. A number of studies and surveys are being regularly carried out. One notable study covering leading CEOs and deans of business schools in the US has provided very valuable results. A notable majority of the deans have declared that Humor can reduce executive stress significantly. The CEOs were unanimous in stating that Humor is not merely desirable in business; it plays such an important role in today's business environment that special attention should be paid by executives to improve their Sense of Humor. They have also suggested that while recruiting, applicants with better Sense of Humor may be given preference, when other eligibility factors are equal. Another survey of CEOs highlighted the fact that most of the highly successful CEOs have already imbibed Humor into their leadership mode.

What is Humor? It is a way of looking at your environment, your people, and yourself. By focusing attention on the positive side of the above, Humor enables you to take failures and disappointments in your stride without getting unduly depressed. When you use Humor while interacting with people, it is necessary that it stands on the foundation of mutual respect. Humor, for it to be successful, has to have an element of surprise implanted in it. It should be relevant and should contain some truth. These features make everyone pleasant and relaxed. By using Humor you are empowering your people to get closer to you. The forms in which Humor can be displayed are many. An attempt has been made to introduce some of the popular modes of laughter in this book.

Subtle Humor

☺ *A very successful project manager called his men to his cabin and said, "Friends, I've got some good news and some bad news. The good news is that we are all working late tonight to make the hydraulic test rig for HAL ready for dispatch before sunrise. The bad news is, I'm making coffee for us all!"*

You see that the manager used subtle Humor to convey that the group had to work all night and finish the job. This goes to show that Humor need not prompt you to shirk any of your responsibilities. You can be a tough taskmaster and still have fun with your team.

Bob Ross has this to say on corporate leadership with Humor:

"We can get anything done by one of the only three options we have: Bullying, Buying off, or Beguiling. The first two are less desirable methods, because they leave behind unhealthy after-effects. Humor comes very handy in Beguiling, which is using our charm with the person; it's subtle and sensitive. It improves the mutual relationship and promotes an intense zeal to complete common goals" (Ross 1992).

A Teacher's Experience

☺ *A friend of mine, a teacher, shared the following experience with me. Usually she and her colleagues met in the school lounge every morning for a gossip session in the short interval just before the commencement of classes. The gossip would generally be denouncing either the principal or any of their colleagues, who were not present. This routine used to put all of them, without their awareness, into a negative mood. My friend felt so drained out everyday that teaching in the first period was a veritable ordeal for her. One day she was late to school and so missed the gossip session; but she was surprised that she felt a new zeal while taking the first hour of class. She subsequently regularly missed the lounge meetings and found a new joy in teaching. She shared this experience with her friends, some of whom experimented on their own and had a similar pleasant experience. They reviewed their usual routine and found that it was necessary to pepper their lounge meetings with Humor. They thus started sharing jokes, cartoons, funny stories, etc., with each other on a daily basis.*

Teamwork with Humor

☺ *A friend of mine who regularly acts in television serials invited me to witness the shooting of an episode one Sunday. I accepted the invitation and was very happy about it. A great surprise was in store for me that day, to find such an enjoyable atmosphere with so many people busy in making arrangements for the serial's shooting. Everyone was busy the entire day, busy in their respective areas of work, and at the same time having non-stop fun. They hurriedly snatched some snacks from the cafeteria and gulped their tea, without stalling the ongoing work. It was very difficult for me to find out who the boss was! It was very clear that the people there were very productive, clicked like a champion team, and also enjoyed their work.*

Inspired Salesgirl!

☺ *I was once in a departmental store in Bangalore and was impressed by the quality of service the salesgirls provided to the customers. I saw a Marwari woman there who asked the attendant in the fruit section for half a jackfruit. The salesgirl told the woman that only full jackfruits were sold. The woman raised her voice and insisted on buying a half fruit. So the salesgirl asked the woman to wait for a minute and went to the assistant manager of the store. She said to him, "There's this big-mouthed Marwari woman who wants to buy half a jackfruit ...." Just then she noticed the Marwari woman standing three feet away, staring at both of them. Immediately, the salesgirl added, "and this lady here wants to buy the other half!"*

Such ready wit and presence of mind can only be found in employees who are motivated and not driven. Humor is a whisper from the soul, imploring the mind and body to relax, to let go and be at peace again. There is health and happiness in the mirth in which an honest laugh takes birth. Of all of God's gifts to man, laughter is one of the most subtle and most precious. It has neither religion nor caste; and no language barrier either. As an equalizer, it is unparalled.

Today, people in business organizations experience greater levels of anxiety, tension, risk, discontent and bitterness, which are the result of the feverish rivalry that exists in the business environment. A continuous need to boost profitability is forcing companies to take recourse to cutbacks, redundancy, amalgamations, takeovers, etc., which tend to worsen the corporate environment. Obviously, the external forces resulting out of market dynamics are beyond one's control. Their impact on the health and happenings in the company is also inevitable. But the manner in which managers look at things, their understanding of the situation, and their response to it, are totally within the power of the company management. The step-ladder structure of the organizations and the inter-company, inter-departmental, and personal rivalry spirit which preoccupies them, make the employees nervous, watchful, and suspicious; their interactions cannot be free, frank, and extempore. Employees, in their zeal to endorse their status, function, and façade, are very likely to become more self-centered, adamant, unfriendly, and secretive.

As some of the employees rise high in the management hierarchy, they distance themselves from the vast majority of working-level people. As a result, the higher management is cut off from first-hand information about ground realities on the shopfloor and marketplace. The information they receive through their deputies may be in variance with actual facts. In order to overcome this handicap, the managers have to focus on building a candid atmosphere around them.

The current business environment has brought in one more important social change. Today, many job seekers are required to live away from their parents and relatives. They are also required to change their jobs quite frequently. Usually their family sizes are limited to husband, wife and child. So when employees are overwhelmed emotionally, they have very limited outlets. This makes it compulsory for them to seek such outlets in their co-employees and immediate boss. Their needs are fulfilled only if there is a feeling of camaraderie among these people.

Managers, therefore, have a formidable responsibility: they have to recognize these trends and discover ways and means of preventing premature burn-outs of their people. In addition, they have to simultaneously augment employee effectiveness and company profits. Recent experience has proved that this goal can be achieved by encouraging teamwork, mutual respect, empathy, and zeal for achieving.

Humor has been used by many managers to generate a favorable ambience at the workplace. They can use Humor to enliven their communications, presentations, instructions, and appreciations, Humor can stimulate employees in meetings. Properly applied Humor enables people to unwind, get energized and reach their goals. Humor keeps employees happy at work, helps them take up their responsibilities without getting too tense, and to create an atmosphere of friendship with others by reducing unwanted rivalry and bickering. Humor is a strong remedy for tension. It helps an individual to find joy even in adverse conditions by overcoming the emotions of despair and vulnerability. The greatest benefit of Humor lies in the fact that it does not call for any big capital investment or special off-job training. It is applicable at all locations and by all people.

Today's managers are in dire need of the added advantages that Humor confers. Irrespective of your position in the hierarchy, you stand to profit by using this important resource. The more different you are from your employees in seniority, experience, training, learning, refinement, taste, sophistication, etc., the more useful Humor would be to you in bridging this disparity.

An intimate household, a match-winning sports team, a prosperous enterprise, all of these have one similar attribute: the team members take pleasure in the company of one another, in amusing themselves, while simultaneously achieving their respective goals. The cultivation of Humor does not lead to loss of rank in the organization, it does not call for reduction of any responsibilities or authority; you need not violate any company code to use Humor. You would not lose the respect of your assistants or the regard of your superiors by using Humor.

Humor is a skill which can be learnt and improved upon by anyone who decides to do so; you can be sure of reaping rich dividends for your efforts to master this skill, because you will stand tall in any crowd. Your guidance will be valued by everyone and the armor of Humor will shield you from any attack.

Henry Ford

☺ *The authoritative style of management is certainly a thing of the past. When a manager at Ford Motors expressed disagreement with what Henry Ford said, the latter said to the manager, "Let's go outside to see whose name is on the building!"*

Samuel Goldwyn

☺ *In a similar style, Samuel Goldwyn, the Hollywood film magnate said, "I don't want any 'Yes' men around me. I want everyone to tell me the truth, even if they have to lose their jobs!"*

J. R. D. Tata

☺ *Fortunately such an autocratic style of management has given way to more consultative and participative management styles. If in any meeting everyone agreed on any of his proposals, J.R.D. Tata, the doyen of Tata group of Industries, would postpone taking a final decision on the matter to the next meeting. His principle was that if everyone agrees so readily, the subject has not been understood fully. That was J.R.D's way of encouraging dissent and frankness!*

Sense of Humor enables you to view situations from different perspectives. This will enable you to discover a number of solutions to the problems you face, giving you the privilege to choose the best.

FIGURE 4
Mind Your Manners!

Jargon Helps!

☺ *The statistics department of a south Indian university was required to procure about a hundred pairs of dice for their experimental studies. When they put in their requisition, it was rejected by the purchase committee, who thought a gambling device should have no place in their university. An assistant in the statistics department made some alterations in the purchase requisition and resubmitted it. This time the request was approved. The new requisition was for, "multiple sets of cubic random-number generators!"*

Reframing anything in a humorous way can help disguise repulsive situations or unfavorable news in a much more acceptable manner. What was once called a garbage heap is now called reclaimed property. Airlines call the "life jacket" a "personal flotation device" and so on.

Make New Mistakes!

☺ *Bhise, the newly recruited wireman came out of the boss's cabin crestfallen; it appeared that the boss had literally chewed him raw! Bhise was almost in tears. Pawar the veteran electrician consoled Bhise: "Ganya, you should not take boss's words so seriously. The boss finds fault with everyone. I saw him the other day taking Santa Claus to task at the Christmas party; he insisted that Santa should shave, slim down, and wear a more sober outfit! I'll tell you the boss is good at heart. Once you start doing good work, he'll pat you on the back. What you should do now is to not make the same mistakes; make new ones!" Both of them laughed loudly.*

Bhise stayed on and moved on to become an asset to the company.

MD Quotes Bible

☺ *A polyester manufacturing company had received a notice from the public health authorities that they needed to strictly abide by the recently amended norms on pollution control. The matter was urgent and serious. Failure to meet the deadline was an invitation to heavy penalties. So the MD called a meeting of the senior executives to find a solution. Even after hours of discussion, no satisfactory solution was reached. The VP (processes) finally had this to say: "Our problem is similar to the one faced by the Biblical hero Moses. Moses, the Hebrew prophet, led the Israelites out of Egyptian slavery; the Egyptian army was chasing Moses, who, when he came near the Red Sea, didn't know how to cross it. He fervently prayed to God to rescue his people. He heard the divine voice which spelt out the good news and the bad news. The good news was that the Red Sea would be parted for Moses's people to pass through, but the bad news was that Moses should file an environmental consequences report, the next day!"*

The group had a hearty laugh; when they returned to the business of the meeting, the re-energized minds came out with many useful ideas to solve the problem.

Theory and Practice!

☺ *A garment manufacturing company in Bangalore signed a contract with an overseas marketing agency to export shirts* to the stipulations of the overseas client. To achieve this, a new plant and certain new equipment were installed. There were a number of changes in the methods of manufacturing, based on time and motion study. The head of the industrial engineering division was presenting to the supervisors of the manufacturing departments, the advantages of the new system. He explained how the changes were inevitable and yet how those very changes are resisted by the people in the beginning. At the end, he said, "I would like to share with you my own experience at home, when I applied time and motion study principles." So saying he presented a case study of his wife's procedure for preparing the daily breakfast and put forward the results to the group.

"When I observed my wife's activities for a couple of days, I was convinced that my wife's methods were stealing her valuable time and stamina. I recorded the number of trips she made from the kitchen to the dining room, carrying each time a single piece; I recommended that she should, in future, carry many more items at a time."

"Did it work?" asked the curious group in unison.

"Sure, it did" replied the head. "Instead of my wife taking 30 minutes to prepare the breakfast, it is now taking me just 10 minutes!"

Accountability vs Authority!

☺ Mr Koushik was the in-charge of the personnel department and a Swedish engineer the then technical manager of a re-puted bearing company in Maharashtra. The manufacturing plant was on a piece of land of about 12 acres in area. Metal scrap, packing boxes, and other such materials were lying about on the vacant portions of the land. Only the built-up area had been protected by fencing. One day, the technical manager who was surveying the property was aghast to see a bitch and its five puppies in the middle of the packing boxes. He flew into a rage and shouted, "Who has allowed this bitch inside? What are the security staff doing?"

Mr Koushik was informed about this by the frightened security supervisor. The former met the technical manager and said, "Sir, I understand your feelings. That bitch and the puppies there, certainly have no place on our property. But sir, your questioning creates a situation of accountability far in excess of authority!"

These words made the technical manager laugh out loud. He said, "Mr Koushik, I understand what you're hinting at. I remember your repeated suggestion to fence the whole area, which has not been so far sanctioned. Okay, you'll have the sanction today itself. Go ahead and get the land fenced on all sides."

—Satish Koushik

Conclusion

Humor is not a substitute for any management technique or a cure-all for the failures of the enterprise. Humor at the workplace is much more than the telling of side-splitting stories or the giving of light-hearted lectures. It is creating a work atmosphere which is constructive and creative, practical and pragmatic, enthusiastic and effective. It is about mobilizing the benefits of playfulness and pleasure to bring out the finest in your people and yourself.

Chapter 3

Programming Yourself for Humor

"I realize that Humor isn't for everyone; it's only for people who want to have fun, enjoy life and feel alive."

— Anne Wilson Schaef

A vast majority of people are scared of Humor. They complain in chorus:

"I'm not funny."
"Humor is beyond my reach."
"I'm not cut out for jokes."
"I'm not quick-witted."
"I don't have a comical personality."
"I'm not sharp."
"My memory is poor. I can't recall jokes."
"Whenever I try to tell a joke, it fails."
"Humor isn't my cup of tea."

When people voice such feelings, these are usually their genuine, wholehearted perceptions; there's no doubt about it. The famous British actor Edmund Kean, on his deathbed, endorsed these views by saying, "Dying is easy; comedy is difficult!"

However, these apprehensions and perceptions that people have about their weaknesses need not cause any alarm as they are not true. When you think you cannot tell a joke, this thought of yours is premature; the real fact is, you can tell a joke. For that matter, almost everyone can. Then why do people fail? Mostly because they give up too quickly; they withdraw from the stage too fast; they leave the arena without giving themselves a fair chance to succeed. The child who wants to learn cycling cannot afford to quit cycling just because he/she fell down and bruised his/her knees in the initial attempt. The youth who wants to become a boxer should not leave the ring as soon as he has had his first black eye.

Do you remember how you learnt to swim? Perhaps you wanted to learn to swim only because you envied your friends when they bragged about how they enjoyed themselves at the swimming pool. It is possible that when you visited the pool for the first time you were quite scared of the water and that you cursed yourself for harboring any thoughts of swimming. How many times did you think of running away from the place, of forgetting everything to do with swimming? Your first plunge into the water only aggravated your fears, as water rushed into your nostrils and had you coughing, choking, croaking, and wheezing. A number of people do quit swimming after such an experience on the first day. But you did not give up so quickly. Perhaps your parents either coerced or cajoled you into continuing with your swimming lessons; or you were compelled to match your friends who bragged to you the other day! You sought the guidance and support of the coach at the pool; you observed other swimmers at the pool, synchronising the movements of their body and limbs; you experimented and learnt how easy and effortless it was to float in water. This helped you lose all your fear of water. Gradually, you learnt the different strokes, the kicks and dives, and experienced the fun, enjoyment, and excitement of swimming. It is exactly the same way with Humor. (If you're not a swimmer, you can recollect how you learnt driving, or how you mastered tennis, or contract bridge.) If you apply the same patience and perseverance to being humorous you can certainly display Humor, because Humor is in no way more difficult than learning any other skill like golf, oratory, singing, painting, etc.

You can certainly tell a joke, because telling a joke does not call for any extraordinary intellect or genius. If you, as a manager, are successful everyday in convincing your customer to buy a product or service, in persuading your boss to accept your idea for cost reduction, in inspiring your assistants and colleagues to improve quality and productivity, in proving to the statutory authorities that their objections and reservations about your company's activities were unreasonable and uncalled for, you most certainly can tell a joke with much less effort. But you have to let go of any negative thoughts covering your ability to do so. For your Humor to succeed, you have to try with all your might. Your efforts should be full of enthusiasm, earnestness, and the intense desire to succeed. In short, the Sense of Humor is an attitude. Any new perspective can be acquired to replace an earlier one. No human being is born with a Sense of Humor. Every humorist has learnt Humor with his or her efforts. Cary Grant, the famous Hollywood actor, explained his methodology: he made every effort to emulate the few persons he sincerely admired and respected. This role-modeling technique has been used by several humorists and it is a very effective tool to developing almost any skill or attitude.

Did you say that you cannot remember jokes? Be honest with yourself. You are not usually hard-pressed for time when preparing for your presentations. That preparation time is more than adequate for you to add a dash of Humor to your presentation material. You don't have to write full-length humorous skits; all that is required is to add to your talk a comic citation, a funny fable or an amusing anecdote to embellish the ideas and arguments you put forward. You are required to make all these preparations so that you are your natural self while making the presentation and your Humor also comes forth spontaneously. You can, of course, carry your notes with you, so that in the most unlikely event that you don't recall your points, you can refer to your notes and hence never panic. Moreover, you must remember that you are not trying to hold a fun-filled, 90-minute comedy like a professional comedian. You're not required to, that's not your job. You're a business manager trying to make the points you're putting forward more effective and memorable.

You may now ask: "If it is so simple and straightforward, why are people so scared of Humor? Why do most of your friends and colleagues say that Humor is pretty dangerous?" These are good questions and it is good that you are keen to know the answers. Humor is very potent and forceful. It is similar to fire or electricity. If misused, Humor can be vicious. Bad Humor can hurt people deeply. So you have to be cautious while using Humor. Do you run away from electricity just because you have to be cautious when you use it? Never. You make sure that all precautions are taken; you provide yourself an ample safety margin; you make electrical installations idiot-proof.

After taking all these steps, you are free from any danger of being electrocuted whenever you switch on a light, the television, or your air-conditioner. If something goes wrong, you switch off the power immediately before attending to the fault. In exactly the same manner, you have to first understand in what way Humor can become dangerous and then take the necessary steps to prevent such a situation.

FIGURE 5
Humor is for Everyone!

Dangerous Humor will be discussed in detail in Chapter 8, with illustrations. It is, however, relevant at this point for you to know about the two main causes for harmful Humor: vindictiveness and zero awareness, and of the two vindictiveness is more common. The vindictive or vengeful use of Humor involves teasing, insulting, and provoking others by speaking disrespectfully and sarcastically. Such a form of Humor is very likely to build up rivalry, hostility, and alienation. Taunts, mockery, curses, etc., fall under this category. The only way to prevent such undesirable results is by avoiding such Humor totally.

The lack of awareness poses a more difficult problem. Vindictive Humor is put into use by you only with your express approval; it cannot happen without your knowledge. On the other hand, Humor of the zero awareness category is used by you without you knowing all the facts. Your Humor, however, hurts the listeners and you may be unaware of this too. Imagine the following scenario: there is a death in the family of one of your assistants and when he reports to duty after being absent for a couple of days, you ask him, "How was your second honeymoon?"

Of course, you would never have said such a thing had you known about the loss suffered by your assistant. So, a little precaution can generally save you from such an embarrassing situation. Before using Humor, make it a point to know something about your listeners. Put yourself in their position and determine whether the Humor you plan to employ would be welcome to you. This simple test could help you avoid using possibly offensive Humor caused by lack of awareness.

Humor Calls for Homework

You may wonder about the secret behind the success of celebrities like Wimbledon tennis champion Roger Federer, Indian chess wizard Vishwanathan Anand, or the great American humorist Bob Hope. All these eminent personalities would be unanimous in saying that commitment and hard work are the foundations of their success. Your success in using Humor also calls for these attributes. Your Humor will be highly effective when it looks amusing, brilliant, extempore, smooth, elegant, and informal. Perhaps you have already appreciated many of these features in the Humor of your role model. Be rest assured that your role model has put in enormous amounts of preparation and planning to reach his/her current state of perfection. You are also required to explore, experiment, enquire, evaluate, prepare, practice, and review. You must, however, remember that this prescription only looks formidable at first sight, yet, you will enjoy it as you walk through the various stages. The rewards you will beget from Humor are fabulous. In addition, they are fair, frank, forthright, fast, and forthwith. Laughter, which is the appreciative acknowledgement by the listeners of your Humor, can neither be faked nor camouflaged. The reward for your hard work is that you have the full attention of your listeners, your message will be well received, and there's a strong possibility that your viewpoint will be given fair consideration. What more can you expect?

Blueprint to Banish Humor Phobia

Anyone who has at any time laughed or smiled can learn to use Humor, successfully. The course of action detailed ahead becomes very useful while taking a methodical approach to Humor.

Be Sincere

Your progress is directly proportional to your sincerity and your commitment. Your interest in your people has to be genuine, then only can you start getting their viewpoint. The viewpoint of others will give you insight not only into your presentation, but also to the type and extent of Humor you should employ. Your own mood, your attitude, your appearance and your interest are very important factors in making your communication effective, because your listeners generally reflect your own attributes. So be relaxed, wear a smile, and display warmth.

Proceed Slowly

It is prudent to overcome your fear of Humor little by little. So decide to include just one joke or anecdote in your next presentation. Overcome the temptation to pack it with all the funny stories you heard at your club last week. Focus on making that one piece of Humor fully effective. When you've succeeded in getting the laughter in the manner you expected, you can include two more humorous stories in your next presentation; you can then move on for more, step by step. Remember how you approached the swimming pool last Sunday when it was very cold: you went in feet first, then down till the water reached your knees, then slowly up to your waist level, and when that was agreeable, you plunged in!

Search for the Story

In order to include that one special item of Humor in your presentation, search for it in all the sources of Humor available to you. Recall funny incidents from your past, go through the collection of anecdotes you have amassed, glance through books of quotations and one-liners bought last year, peep into those joke books borrowed from the library; select about a dozen pieces of Humor which appeal to you most and study them.

Polish the Pot-pourri

Review the collected items and rank them on the basis of relevance, appropriateness, and effectiveness. Be warned, even the item you rank highest will not allow itself to be included into your presentation in its "as is" condition. Modify it, change its language, alter the names of persons and places, replace the time or period detailed therein to make it sound relevant, cut down the length or elaborate additional details to suit your purpose, and take whatever liberty that is required to metamorphose the item to suit your needs.

Practice to Perform

When you are satisfied that the joke you have recast looks like your story, you have to learn to articulate it. Stand before a tall mirror and speak out loudly; don't read it out. Check whether you feel comfortable while delivering the jokes; make sure your expression, gestures, and body language are in tune with what you say. Repeat this performance a number of times till you are sure you have mastered your humorous anecdote.

Use it Again and Again

Now that you have perfected your "funny story," use every opportunity to deliver it to your family, friends, and deputies. Seek feedback from your listeners on every occasion. Observe and mentally record their immediate responses while delivering the anecdote/joke. You will notice that with every rehearsal you shall be tempted to make some modifications to the story. This means your story becomes more refined and powerful, and you become more self-assured. You can now repeat this entire procedure with another story and so on. Slowly, you can enlarge the collection of your own Humor and also get rid of your Humor phobia.

Sense of Humor = Proper Perspective

Business people can benefit by adopting Sense of Humor in a big way. It can save them from doing things foolishly!

Of course, it can also save others from such foolish acts, but the cost of foolishness in business would be enormous and that is why these applications are being highlighted here.

Example 1

☺ *Prakash (not his real name) and I had joined the company as graduate engineering probationers at the same time; to be very precise, he had joined three months earlier. Prakash was a very talented person. In addition to having had a bright academic career, he was a gifted orator and singer, and could act well on the stage. He personally knew many accomplished artists from these fields. Did all these qualifications give him joy? Not at all! He was seething constantly, believing he deserved much more than what he was getting. The company promoted him every three years and after seven years of service made him responsible for the Research and Development Division. This should have made Prakash jubilant; in fact he was happy till he came to know that I was also given a similar salary hike and was given charge of Planning and Production Control. This news robbed him of all his joy. He went to the works manager with a complaint that the company had grossly neglected his achievements. Within a couple of weeks he resigned and left the company to join a competitor. There too Prakash felt that the authority given to him was too low to match his competence; he quarreled with the management and left the job in a huff.*

A Sense of Humor could have helped Prakash a great deal. He and his family would have been much better off had he not drawn the wrong conclusions about his status and future in the first company. Sense of Humor teaches you sound logic and prevents you from throwing the baby out along with the bath water while you're cleaning the bathtub.

Example 2

☺ An incident in the life of President Abraham Lincoln is worthy of attention at this point. In the days when Abraham Lincoln was practicing law there was a court case going on. A motorboat plying in the Mississippi river had caused some damage to a newly built railway bridge. The railway authorities had sued the motorboat owner in the hope of recovering a big sum to cover the cost of repairs. They hired a number of eminent lawyers who presented their case with great polish and made a favorable impression on the jury. The motorboat owner, on the other hand, hired only Lincoln to defend him. At last, the arguments came to an end. There was a lunch break after which the defense had to make their concluding remarks to be followed by the announcement of the verdict by the jury. During the lunch interval, Lincoln approached the jury and told them a story about a farmer. One evening, the farmer's eight-year-old son came running to him and said, "Dad, come quickly. Mary [the boy's sister] and the new helper are up on the heap of grass. Her skirt is raised and his pants are down. If you don't hurry, all our grass will get soaked in their pee!"

The father said, "Son, you've got the facts right, but you've reached the wrong conclusions."

When the court resumed, Lincoln, in his closing argument, said, "The learned defense lawyers have presented an impressive case. They have their facts absolutely right, but they have reached totally wrong conclusions."

> *The jurors laughed loudly and after a recess returned to give the verdict in favor of the boat owner.*

Sense of Humor consists of three important attributes:

1) Capacity to identify the facts as they are.
2) Competence to realize the truth as it is.
3) Aptitude to respect reality as it stands.

In Prakash's case, he failed in all the three counts. He did not identify the facts. He did not see that the company considered him to be a big asset. He had been given the highest salary hikes; he was given maximum promotions. The complete responsibility of running a vitally important function like research and development was offered to him. It was an excellent opportunity for him, both for self-development and for gaining prestige in public. Prakash did not identify these facts because he was blinded by his extreme ego. In addition, he craved not so much to get more for himself, but to get more than all the others. He also did not realize the truth. A growing company cannot be run by one divisional head; it needs a number of talented persons to manage the several main divisions like R&D, engineering, production, marketing, purchase, personnel, quality, and so on. Prakash could not respect this reality, the reality that some of his colleagues could be equal to him (if not superior) in competence.

Some Sense of Humor would have prompted him to recognize that he had got a wonderful opportunity to prove his worth to the company and to enrich his own potential as a professional research engineer. He had the scope to travel far and wide, in both India and abroad. His division had been given priority in budgetary provisions. So, even though he and a couple of his colleagues shared the same status in the company, he was the more likely one to overtake the rest in the years to come, by dint of his valuable contributions to the company. All these realizations would have made Prakash a happy, enthusiastic, and committed manager instead of a frustrated and angry young man.

Example 3

☺ *The general manager of an Indian engineering company, Balaji (name changed), was on a visit to Europe in late 1957 to finalize a collaboration for their product line "A" with some leading European company. There were about a dozen companies in the running, but essentially the choice had been narrowed down to two companies—one Swiss and another West German. Balaji happened to visit Switzerland first. The host company there had sent a limousine to Zurich airport along with a very senior executive to receive Balaji and take him to the luxurious hotel where reservations had been made. When Balaji visited the company plant the next morning he was welcomed by one of the directors of the company who also entertained Balaji for lunch. The plant visit was quite impressive because of the very sophisticated equipments which were under manufacture. But there were very few components of the product line "A" on the shopfloor. Balaji was, however, shown a short film detailing how these products were made and tested.*

After a couple of days Balaji visited the West German company. They had booked Balaji into a modest hotel quite close to their plant. As there was no one to receive him at the airport on his arrival (that day being a Sunday), Balaji took a taxi at the airport and reached the hotel. The next morning, a marketing officer of the company called on Balaji and took him to the plant where Balaji was given a very warm welcome. The visit to the manufacturing shops was very illuminating as all the shops were busy in making products of line "A" only.

Balaji returned to India and in his report to his chairman, recommended the Swiss company as the better choice. As later years proved, it was really a very poor choice for the following reasons. The Swiss company was no doubt a mega company of international fame, but as far as products of line "A" were concerned, their design was at least 20 years old. The company had stopped R&D activities of these products a number of years ago and was contemplating stopping their manufacture too. The revenue of Line "A" products was less than 8 percent of the total revenue of the company during the previous year.

The German company was a sharp contrast; it was neither as big nor as famous as the Swiss one. But it was the world leader as far as product line "A" was concerned. Line "A" products accounted for more than 75 percent of the total annual revenue of this company. A large number of R&D projects were under various stages of completion, signifying the total commitment of this company to product line "A". The Germans were keen to enter India. When their company was not chosen for collaboration, they set up a company in India, on their own, and became a serious competitor to Balaji's company.

If Balaji had the correct attitude and perspective, he would have identified the above facts, realized the truth, and respected the reality. He would have given a lot more importance to the commitment and technical superiority of the Germans coupled with their keenness to enter the Indian market, than *to the hospitality score of the Swiss company. This step would not only have given his company products of more modern design, but would also have eliminated a stiff competitor in the Indian marketplace.*

Example 4

☺ *Stephen Covey, the author of the famous book,* The 7 Habits of Highly Effective People, *writes about an American company whose president invited Covey to help him. The president had a serious complaint, that his people did not cooperate with him and that his company was going to be in the red. Covey studied the situation and found the employees to be totally noncooperative. He also discovered that the president had made an announcement at the beginning of the fiscal year, that the company would reward the manager whose department was most productive during the year with a one week, all expenses paid trip for him and his family to Bermuda. Covey found that it was this gimmick which had caused the problem. With this holiday incentive the president had introduced competition among the departments, while for getting good corporate results cooperation is vitally important. Covey suggested a new system of rewards focusing on personal and organizational excellence, which gave priority to cooperation among the departments. The president was pleasantly surprised to see a complete change for the better in the attitude of his people.*

The president had not identified the fact that for better corporate results, close cooperation among all departments was essential. He had not realized the truth that his reward scheme caused competition among departments which was detrimental to cooperation. He also failed to respect the reality that the scheme could create just one winner and 459 losers in the company.

It was necessary to change this vicious perspective, and that was what Covey did.

Sense of Humor is seeing the reality, recognizing the truth, and using your judgement to respect the truth. There is a cycle of mutual benefit at play when you use Sense of Humor. Because of your better judgement you become more constructive and helpful. These qualities in turn augment your Sense of Humor. Such a chain of benefits is yours to keep in your personal life as well as in business. The results in business applications are simply mind-boggling. You just cannot afford to overlook them.

Conclusion

Humor is available to everyone, irrespective of age, gender, color, race, or size; there is no need for changing your dress, voice, intonation, language, or gestures to use Humor. In fact, it is all the more important that you be yourself to succeed with Humor. Remember that you're unique and you are advised to derive maximum leverage out of this uniqueness. Programming yourself for Humor really emphasizes that you should not renounce your true self and try to become someone else in order to be humorous. This is the key to enjoying Humor and becoming successful.

Chapter 4

Laughing at Yourself!

"You've an advantage; you can laugh at yourself first and beat any other, who wants to do so, to the second place!"

Making fun of yourself in the presence of others leads to guaranteed all-round cheerfulness, laughter, and acclamation. This technique is simple, straightforward, and undemanding. This is the reason why a large number of celebrities can be seen to have mastered this type of Humor. Ethel Barrymore has gone on record saying that a person grows up the day he has his first real laugh, at himself. Truly blessed are they who can laugh at themselves, for they shall never cease to be amused.

This highest form of Humor consists of you pointing a finger at yourself and laughing in the presence of others. This quality will endear you to the people you are with. They will feel relaxed as the Humor will not target them and they, in the safety of that invulnerability, will find themselves free to laugh heartily with you. It is for this very same reason they are attracted to you too. They will feel a sense of relief and satisfaction to find you have some weakness so they can equate you with themselves and this in turn will breed a familiarity which makes them love you. They will also see that by laughing at yourself you have displayed a sense of total self-assurance; you're not afraid of owning up to any imperfection or frailty because you are sure of your mettle and might. According to Humor expert Malcolm Kushner, even though you appear to put yourself down, you are in fact building yourself up. In this manner, self-directed Humor enhances mutual affinity, creates empathy, and leads to harmony and accord.

The team spirit rises a couple of notches and the determination grows as never before. Study the following examples.

Woodrow Wilson

☺ *Woodrow Wilson, the US President, used to say: "When I was studying, everyone could get university degrees. Take the case of my friend; he had three degrees; the third was given because he already had two, the second because he had only one and the first because he had none!"*

Greater than Einstein

☺ *A distinguished mathematics professor in Mysore University used to jocularly claim, "Most of you don't know this fact: 'I'm greater than Einstein. Do you know why?' It is said that 12 persons understood Einstein, when he spoke. But when I speak, none of you understand me!"*

Robert Orben

☺ *Robert Orben used to remark, "Every morning I get up and look through the Forbes list of the richest people in America. If I am not there, I go to work!"*

Steve Martin

☺ *Steve Martin was ailing in a hospital when a friend visited him. Martin was confiding in him with a big triumphant* smile, *"The doctor just now told me the good news that I was suffering from a disease named after me!"*

Lincoln on Marriage

☺ *Abraham Lincoln used to say, long after his marriage, "I have come to the conclusion never again to think of marrying, and for this reason I can never be satisfied with anyone who would be blockheaded enough to have me!"*

Robert Benchley

☺ *Robert Benchley, the humorist would often say, "I won't trust a bank that would lend money to such a poor risk as me!"*

W.C. Fields

☺ *W.C. Fields said, "I'm free of all prejudices; I hate everyone equally!"*

Calvin Coolidge

☺ *When asked what he did for exercise, US President Calvin Coolidge said, "Having my picture taken!"*

Lyndon Johnson

☺ *When US President Lyndon Johnson was asked by a reporter what his golf handicap was, Johnson replied, "I don't have any handicap; I am all handicap!"*

Barbara Bush

☺ *The US first lady Mrs Barbara Bush, after leaving the White House, used to say that she never agreed with the fashion specialists who found fault with her dresses— "The simple truth is my dresses are great; it's me who doesn't look so good!"*

Making Fortunes!

☺ *A highly successful Indian industrial house had an idea to set up factories in Malaysia. So, a team consisting of the company's top persons visited Kuala Lumpur and met with several people there. When they sought the guidance of some Indian businessmen who had already tried to set up their branches there, they unanimously gave this advice, "The one and only sure way of making a small fortune out of a business in Malaysia is to come with a larger fortune!"*

Laxmanrao Kirloskar

☺ *Laxmanrao Kirloskar (LKK), the founder of Kirloskar Group of Industries, to whom industry in India owes so much, started with very modest means. By dint of his technical acumen, simple living, principle-centredness, and hard work he could set up many large companies which could give employment to thousands of villagers, in spite of the hurdles posed by the British Raj. But whenever anyone admired Laxmanrao, he would say: "Whatever you may say, my mother-in-law is not happy. She wanted her daughter to marry a Tehsildar or a higher ranking officer. Now she is unluckily married to a 'ghisadi' (a labourer in a foundry).*

So you see, I'm only a ghisadi." By refraining to put himself
on a pedestal and by sharing the above family drama, LKK
became very dear to all the people. He was addressed by all
the workers and their family members as "Papa."

Breaking Even!

☺ *In 1986, we started a private limited company, with each
family member contributing his might towards the company's
capital, and started manufacturing some engineering equipment. When the first year was over all the family members
were eager to know how the firm had performed. My
own curiosity was also mounting every day, as I was the
senior-most family member involved. I had asked our
accountant to give the financial statements as soon as they
were ready, to me only, because I wanted to have the privilege
of informing the other stakeholders the results personally.*

*One late evening, my accountant rang me up and by the
tone of his voice I knew he was very excited. He gave me
the good news that the bottom-line was black. I was very
happy with this news and I asked him to make a dozen
copies of the financial statements and send them to all the
directors, and also to our bankers. The voice at the other end
grew very weak. I heard our accountant telling me, "If we
buy any computer stationery at this stage, we will end up in
some loss!"*

Third Question

☺ *Sometimes I am invited by cultural organizations to make
humorous speeches. In the beginning, I used to invite a friend*

of mine to accompany me to such functions. By previous arrangement he would ask me two questions to which I had carefully prepared answers. I would receive the questions as if they were impromptu and would go on and give my replies; the replies would provoke peals of laughter in the audience and there onwards, I would get a very good response from the audience.

This practice went on very well for many months. But one day my friend stood up and asked me: "What's the third question you had asked me to ask?"

My Golf!

☺ The other day I went to see my doctor and asked him to help me reduce my weight. (Those days I used to weigh around 90 kg.) The doctor recommended I take up golf as a regular form of exercise. I borrowed a half kit from a friend, enrolled myself as a member of the local golf club (using all my personal influence to get the enrolment), and tried to follow the doctor's advice for a few weeks. Then I discovered that I was not made for that game. I went to see my doctor again and asked him to suggest some other game. But for reasons best known only to him, he insisted that there was no game more effective than golf. Cutting short his speech on the merits of golf I had to tell him this: "Well doctor, please try to understand my problem. Golf may be a good game for you and many others. But as far as I am concerned, it is a miserable ordeal. I placed that stupid ball where I could see, then I could not hit it. Then I placed it where I could hit it; the problem became even worse. I just could not see it. You now tell me what I should do!"

Pursued by Three Companies!

☺ *Raghunath was my classmate while we were studying for our degrees in engineering. We stayed in the same hostel and for two years he was my roommate too. After completing our studies, we took up jobs in different locations and lost contact for years. Then, during one of my visits to Mumbai, I ran into him at a technical seminar. We told each other a number of things. One interesting thing which Raghu told me was about how he got his latest promotion: "I waited for three years but when there was no talk about my salary raise or promotion, I got an appointment with the big boss; there I told him short and straight: 'Boss, I have to know whether you're giving me a raise or not.' The boss asked, 'What's the urgency?' Then I told him, 'I've waited for three years patiently; now there are three companies after me, that's why.' 'Which are these companies?' he asked me. I frankly told him, 'The finance company which has given me a home loan, the telephone company, and the electricity company!' The boss laughed loudly and approved my double promotion along with a hefty salary raise."*

No Tougher Problem

☺ *One day I was discussing the progress of a few projects assigned to me with my boss when some visitors came in. On being introduced we exchanged business cards. While doing so, a photograph fell out of my wallet. My boss picked it up and handed it over to me. After the visitors left, my boss light-heartedly teased me: "Well, even after 30 years of marriage, you're romantic enough to constantly carry your wife's photograph with you. Hearty congratulations!" I made a frank confession, "Mr Gune, it's not because of a romantic outlook that the photo is in my wallet. It serves a different but more important purpose. Whenever I get into a mess, I take a look at the photograph. Immediately I realize that the mess I am in is just nothing when compared to the problem I see in the photograph!"*

Lloyd George

☺ *Lloyd George used to amuse his people by telling them the following story. "'Do you know what happened at the seaside the other day?' A local hero rescued a man who was about to drown in the fiery seawater. Halfway to the shore, the rescuer turned the victim over and stared at his face, before continuing to carry him to the shore. He repeated this process at the shore. The onlookers asked him why he did so. The hero replied, 'Just to make sure that it wasn't Lloyd George!'"*

Retirement

☺ *The company I worked for organized my farewell function to bid me adieu after 36 long years of service. When my turn came to say a few words to suit the occasion, I had this to say, "Retirement from tomorrow means a great thing to me. I will be free to do nothing all day. The important thing to note is that I don't have to turn up at the office to do it."*

George Bernard Shaw

☺ *George Bernard Shaw had this to say about himself, "I was always unlawful; I broke the law when I was born, because my parents were still to be married."*

Help When You Can!

☺ I used to take some pride in helping our children in their homework exercises assigned by the school. My wife would keep on telling me, "Help him when you can, next year he goes into the fifth standard!"

My First Speech

☺ The other day I stood up to give my first public speech on Humor and its many benefits. Somehow, I felt very tense and nervous. I could not say a single word as I felt my mind go blank.

Wiping the perspiration off my brow, I said to the audience, "My dear friends, when I left my house to come here only God and I knew what I planned to say to you, but now it appears that only God knows!"

My words were welcomed by the audience with big applause. This made me lose my nervousness and my amnesia. Soon I could proceed with my speech without any difficulty.

Best Medicine!

☺ I have to be very cautious, when I say, "laughter is the best remedy for all illnesses." Recently, when I visited my friend in Chennai and spoke to a group of people and offered them this advice, my friend's physician filed a legal suit against me for being engaged in medicine without a valid license!

True Feelings!

☺ Albert Einstein, the great physicist, was living in Berlin. He had been invited to attend the wedding ceremony of his friend's daughter. Einstein blessed the new couple and returned home after the wedding. A year later the couple had a baby boy. They visited Einstein with the baby on his first birthday. After the usual pleasantries, Einstein tried to chat with the baby. But as soon as the baby saw the new face, it started crying in its loudest voice. Einstein remarked: "My dear baby, I have come across thousands of people during the last 20 years of my professional life. But you're the first person who honestly conveyed to me how you felt when you saw me!"

So saying Einstein kissed the baby and presented him with a nice toy.

Sam Manekshaw

☺ Field Marshal Sam Manekshaw (Retd.) was the chief strategist and architect of India's victory over Pakistan in the 1971 war for the liberation of Bangladesh.

Once I happened to visit him in Bombay to invite him to be the chief guest for the annual day function of our social club. He readily agreed to our request on one condition. He whispered his condition in my ears, "You should invite my wife too, to the function." We readily agreed to this advice and were happy to do so.

The Field Marshal then explained why he made this special request, "You see, when I was in the army, my wife would see daily that so many persons of the defense services would salute me, the moment they saw me; this made her treat me with respect and awe. But now that I have retired, no one cares to salute me. So in my wife's eyes also, I have lost my stature.

I would like to utilize your invitation to remedy this situation to my benefit. Obviously, when I visit your club as the chief guest, you will honour me, garland me, and say many good things about me. (You may not mean them!) I want that my wife should witness these events so that she may start thinking that her husband still deserves to be respected by her!"

Sir Allen Sheppard

☺ Sir Allen Sheppard, chairman of Grandmet Plc, recommends self-deprecating Humor as a very powerful defense technique. If you happen to err, but are alert enough to own up to the error and laugh at yourself before anyone else can criticize you, you are preempting all such charges. He supports this advice with his own experience. Once he was making an important presentation to a distinguished gathering and inadvertently strayed away from the topic. He continued to speak irrelevantly for quite sometime and the audience started showing signs of restlessness. Sheppard realized his mistake and admitted, "The actual debate was shorter than my summary."

These unexpected words made the audience shake with laughter.

So whenever you happen to make a mistake, instead of trying to conceal it or justify it or play it down, it is highly preferable to ridicule yourself before others have a chance to do so.

Thinking Positively!

☺ An Indian company well-known for the supply of automation systems to defense organizations, received five complaints in *one week from its dissatisfied customers. The managing director called on the customers and said: "We also make it a point to look at the positive side of the situation. You are still on talking terms with us!" With this remark he went on explaining the steps being taken to redress all the complaints.*

Humor of this kind has two kinds of benefits. First, it squashes others' allegations that you are incompetent. Second, you are able to look at your own failures with the most appropriate frame of mind. You can judge things objectively with an open mind.

Correct Prediction

☺ *The chairman of a reputed FMCG manufacturing company was addressing the media representatives after his board meeting in which the financial results of the just-ended year were approved. He said: "Well, ladies and gentlemen, last year I had said that things can't go on like this. And they didn't. They got worse!"*

This piece of Humor, full of surprise and originality, transformed the audience to become highly receptive to what the chairman had to say later, about the causes of the company's under-performance and how the management had geared up to deal with the problems and to assure distinctly superior results during the next year.

Bill Clinton

☺ *Bill Clinton, former President of the United States, had specialized in the art of self-effacing Humor like most other US presidents. When in office he used to remark, "I'm not concerned with my memoirs, but with my resume. You should give me credit for generating, attracting, heightening, and maintaining controversy throughout my eight years as President."*

☺ *When asked what he thought about foreign affairs, Clinton quipped, "Foreign affairs? I don't know, I never had any!"*

George Bush Sr.

☺ *Ex-US President George Bush (Senior) once said, "Ladies and gentlemen, you have to admit that I go in my sentences, where no man has gone before. But in closing, the way I see it, I am a boon to the English language. I've coined new words like 'misunderestimating,' and 'Hispanically.' I've expanded the definition of words themselves, using 'Vulcanized' when I meant 'Polarized,' 'Grecians' when I meant 'Greeks,' 'inebriating' when I wanted to say 'exhilarating,' and instead of 'barriers and tariffs' I said, 'terriers and bariffs'."*

Deeper and Drier!

☺ *Our professor of civil engineering would often ask the students whether they found his lectures boring. Since he was a senior professor who had to be kept happy in order to get good marks in the practical examinations, we would keep telling him his lectures were very interesting. But when he would see our glazed eyes, he would tell us this experience of his: "One day I went to the swimming pool for a nice swim. When I was about to enter the water I could observe a girl student in the final year in our college, accidentally drop her* camera into the pool. Soon she turned to me and said, 'Sir, could you please retrieve my camera?"

"There were many young men swimming, the girl could have asked any one of them who would have gladly obliged her. But the girl had zeroed in on me. So I asked here why she chose me for the job. What she said shocked me. 'Sir, I am your student and as of now I don't know anyone who can go down deeper, stay down longer, and yet come up drier than you!'"

"Since that day, I pay special attention to making my lectures interesting and effective."

Leveling with People!

☺ It was election time and election campaigning was at its peak. One candidate from our local assembly constituency was making his speech. Midway, he inadvertently moved towards the edge of the platform, lost his balance, and fell down. In an instant, he got up and regained his position on the rostrum. He then gave an explanation for this act: "It is essential for all leaders to come down to the level of their people."

Pablo Picasso

☺ Who hasn't heard of Pablo Picasso, the extreme modernist artist? Once, when he was staying in Paris, there was a burglary in his neighborhood. Picasso became curious and joined the crowd of onlookers watching the police at the site of burglary making their investigations. The night watchman there made a sketch of how the burglar looked and gave it to the police. With the help of that sketch the police could arrest the culprit within a week.

Picasso was overwhelmed at the watchman's role. Within a couple of weeks Picasso's own place was burgled. The robber tied Picasso with a rope and made off with some valuables. Picasso wanted to emulate the watchman and so he painted the face of the robber in his own unique way and gave it to the police. The Paris police, with the help of that sketch, were reported to have arrested a total of hundred men and women and also to have confiscated a pair of shoes, a coffin, and a house!

Sarah Bernhardt

☺ *The famous French actress, Sarah Bernhardt, who was the heartthrob of millions of French youth in the prime of her life, had become old. She lived a secluded life staying on the top floor of a multi-storied apartment house. One evening, an 80-year-old man came to meet her. He was exhausted by the time he climbed all the stairs and was panting hard when the actress opened the door for him.*

As soon as he was admitted into the apartment, he asked, "Madame, why do you live in this stupid top floor?"

"Well, I see it this way: by this I can even now make the hearts of men throb and it's the only way I can do it!"

Sharing Your Embarrassments and Laughing

The ability to point a finger at yourself and to laugh is a priceless quality. The world is nearly full of people who take great pleasure in relating their achievements, causing much boredom all around. They earn the neglect and dislike of others. But the person who admits his own frailties, weaknesses, and embarrassments suffered, and who shares the instances in which his foolishness, short-sightedness, or silliness got the better of him, provides unexpected joy to the listeners. The latter will take a special liking to him and become very close. In this way Self-directed Humor (SDH) adds to your appeal and allure in a highly fascinating manner.

An eminent psychiatrist once stated, "I've seldom been called upon to help a person who had a sense of the ridiculous and I've never, never had to treat anyone who could really laugh at himself."

You can appreciate the value attached to SDH by practicing psychiatrists from this statement. Surprisingly, the raw material is available in everyone. What is needed to master this captivating skill is some self-confidence. You should not worry too much about appearing to be foolish for a little while. List the number of amusing little experiences which embarrassed you. Also make a list of your eccentricities and your bizarre habits. Study them and plan how you can relate them to your group by adding a pinch of hilarity and a spark of surprise. You can season it with a little exaggeration. Remember that when you do this, your group will like you for it.

Mark Twain

☺ *Mark Twain had the remarkable ability to poke fun at himself to make his audience roar with laughter. He once said, "Giving up smoking is the easiest thing in the world. I know it because I have done it more than a thousand times!"*

FIGURE 6
Self-directed Humor and Health

George Bernard Shaw

☺ *George Bernard Shaw was approached by a woman (Isodora Duncan) who said to him, "Mr Shaw, I am admired by all for my beauty and you for your intellect. What a wonderful thing it would be, if we have a child—it will have your brain and my beauty!"*

Shaw sent the lady this reply, "How unfortunate it would be if the child takes my beauty and your brain?"

G.B. Shaw

☺ *The first public performance of Shaw's play,* Arms and the Man, *had come to a very successful end. Shaw was invited to come on the stage to receive the applause of the audience. Amidst the din, there came a loud voice, "Come Shaw, come, you know all this stuff is sheer nonsense!" Shaw looked up towards the balcony and called back, "My friend, I know that and I agree with you. But what can we two do against this whole applauding crowd?"*

He Says Only What All Others Say!

☺ *I was a faculty member at a managerial development program organized by a reputed engineering company in Pune. At the end of the program, there was a feedback session. Almost all the 25 participants felt that the program had been very useful. However, one person stood up and said that it was absolutely useless and he had wasted his time in having attended it. The head of the human resources division felt embarrassed. He admonished the young person and asked* him to sit down. He then turned to me, extended his apologies and pleaded: "Sir, you should ignore his words. He is a lazy fool and does not know what he is saying. He cannot think on his own and voices only that which all others say."

Hearing this, I was unable to decide who had embarrassed me more—the young participant or the head of the HR division?

Fact!

☺ On one occasion I had to stay overnight in Mumbai and I didn't have a hotel reservation. I was so weary at the end of the day that I didn't feel like going on an extensive search for a hotel room within my normal budget. Luckily, there was a hotel close to where I was. I went to the reception and enquired about the available accommodation. "What kind of room would you like, sir?" asked the young lady at the reception, beaming.

Somehow, her words encouraged me and I picked up the pen she offered to register myself. As a precaution I asked, "what have you got for around Rs 1,000?"

The young lady replied, "You're holding it, sir!"

The Actress and the Doctor!

☺ Billie Burke, the well-known Hollywood actress was on a trans-Atlantic ocean trip. At dinner, one evening, she observed that the man at the next table appeared to be indisposed. He had a bad cold. She went up to him and asked whether he was in need of any help. The man politely thanked her. The actress became even more sympathetic and gave the *man the following advice, "You're suffering from a cold; I'll tell you what to do for it. Go back to your room and drink plenty of orange juice. Take two aspirins. Cover yourself with two blankets. You'll then sweat a lot and with the sweat your cold will disappear. Take it from me, I know what I'm talking about. I'm Billie Burke from Hollywood."*

The man thankfully smiled, shook hands gratefully and said, "I'm Dr Mayo of the Mayo Clinic."

Not Insulted!

☺ *A seasoned salesman and his junior assistant were chatting. The older man asked the young man about his progress. The junior became sullen and with a choking voice said, "Awful. Wherever I go, I only get severely insulted."*

The veteran responded, "Well, that's strange. I've been a salesman for over 30 years and I've never been insulted. In some places I was not admitted; in some places I was bodily thrown out; in some others the sentries set the dog after me. But I tell you, insulted? Never!"

Andre Agassi!

☺ *"One should not succeed too easily…. Take my own case; I was rewarded too quickly and too early. It made me squander my talent.*

I put in a great deal of work at the buffet table for my achievements—which was, my ranking went down to 140…. To be doing Nike and Canon commercials without ever winning a grand slam left me with a bad rapall image and no substance!"

Mercy, Not Justice!

☺ *The late Professor Zechariah Chafee of Harvard Law School was persuaded by his colleagues to pose for a portrait by artist Gardener Cox. A colleague said, "I hope Cox does you justice."*

    Professor Chafee replied, "What I need is mercy, not justice!"

Shoot First!

☺ *The chief guest was about to start his speech, when a news photographer was observed jockeying for a vantage point, for an action shot. The chairman fearing that the speaker would be annoyed if the photographer flashed the light when he was speaking, called the photographer and said loudly, "Don't shoot while he is speaking. Shoot him before he starts!"*

Real Bravery!

☺ *When he was a brigade commander, Sam Manekshaw was crossing the Sutlej river in a motor launch. The river was in spate and suddenly the outboard motor failed and the boat was sent whirling downstream. There was a waterfall a short distance ahead. So all the occupants of the boat removed their shoes and heavy clothing and jumped into the river in order to swim to safety. But Manekshaw continued to sit erect in the boat, twisting his dark moustache, unconcerned about the impending danger.*

    Just then a chopper sighted the busted boat and rescued its sole occupant. The other officers who had swum to the

*shore safely exclaimed, "How brave of you, sir, to remain so
calm in the face of danger. You didn't even remove your shoes."*

*"For what purpose? There was no use of my jumping
into the river, because I don't know swimming. There was
also no point in asking one of you to take me across, because
the river was raging and it was not easy for you to swim in
unburdened condition; then carrying me would have been a
certain invitation to death."*

Nani Palkhiwala

☺ *Nani Palkhiwala, the eminent jurist, began one of his speeches
with the following statement, "Ladies and gentlemen, I had
to make a choice——whether to deliver a Rolls Royce of a
speech or an Indian car speech. The Rolls Royce speech, like
the engine of that car, is silent and goes on running forever.
This would not suit the present occasion because you all can
spare limited time to listen to my speech. So I would be
delivering an Indian car speech, very loud and shortlived."*

The examples just discussed can give you a start in
practicing self-effacing Humor. You do not need to struggle
hard to make a list of the embarrassments you had, which
can be shared as a part of your SDH. The following
specimens can give you the necessary start.

- You put the letter you had written to your spouse in
  the envelope addressed to the insurance company
  and had it posted.
- It was a momentous event and you wanted to give an
  exceptional performance. Your preparation was

thorough but when you started, you suddenly became a bundle of nerves and cut a sorry figure.

- You had high hopes that the joke you told would get instantaneous applause; but at the crucial time of your punch line, the mike failed; the response you got was less than lukewarm.
- You are negotiating a big deal with your customer. On an important issue your assistant contradicts your statement.
- You have completed an assignment very well. You expect admiration from your boss. But he ignores your achievement and takes you to task regarding a minor slip in some other connection.
- You are to receive a prize on behalf of your department for good safety practices and good housekeeping. While you step on the rostrum to collect the prize, you lose your balance and trip, and have a tear in the seat of your pants.

Initiative from the Top

According to findings by research on organizational dynamics, communication among peers appears to be the easiest, but communication between persons of different ranks usually suffers from want of effectiveness. The rank barrier is a universal felon.

To overcome this it is recommended that Humor should be initiated and encouraged from the top. When the boss uses self-directed Humor, it will encourage the assistants to overcome their apprehensions and to communicate more openly with the boss. So when the rank difference disappears, even temporarily, communication becomes easier, purposeful, and interesting. It will not take a long time for the assistants to emulate the boss in using self-directed Humor as a useful technique; as a result there will be an improvement in the effectiveness of communication and in teamwork.

S.L. Kirloskar

☺ *In 1985, our chairman, Shantanu Kirloskar (popularly known as SLK), visited our plant and office. As he had a keen eye for detail, he wanted to know about the steps taken for recruiting new engineers to the engineering division. Our chief executive, Prabhakar Gune, explained the elaborate process starting with the selection of the top meritorious final semester students at the several good engineering colleges, preexamination campus interviews, written tests, group discussions, and personal interviews. After listening to this narrative, the chairman said, "Mr Gune, I wonder about one thing: if by chance I had to face your selection process, I would not have had even 1 percent chance of getting selected. I remember I was a back-bencher during my college days. While you may scout for talent among meritorious students, keep in mind that talent can also be found in backbenchers!"*

By calling himself a back-bencher, the chairman endeared himself to everyone at the venue and his advice that as trainers we were responsible not only for scouting talent but also for nurturing and developing the available talent with full commitment, attracted immediate acceptance by all of us.

Aptitude Test

☺ *The chief executive, when he reached home, was very weary. He was received by his wife who asked, "You look very tired, dear. Did you have a bad day at the office?"*

CE: "I'm not sure. I took the aptitude test which is given to all the managers, to evaluate them."

Wife: "How did you fare in the test?"

CE: "Don't ask me that, it's good that I own the company!"

No Charges, Lady!

☺ *A lady managing director of a company related the following experience of hers to her vice presidents, "When I reached my hotel from Palam Airport, the taxi driver sighed with relief. When I started to pay his charges, he said to me: "There'll be no charge, lady. You did all the driving!"*

President Lincoln

☺ *One day, President Lincoln had high fever and yet he attended office. There were many visitors there, as usual. The President's doctor, after examining Lincoln declared that he had an attack of measles.*

"Is it infectious?" asked Lincoln.

"Surely, highly infectious," said the doctor.

"Well," said Lincoln with a broad smile, "now I have something I can give to everybody!"

The uniqueness of SDH is that it is a powerful tool which can be put into use by anyone in the organization—from the chairman to the janitor, from the production chief to the trainee helper. When you poke fun at yourself and laugh, you cannot hurt anybody; you are already the winner because you have had a laugh already. The other benefits may or may not materialize but the experiences of a vast number of successful persons clearly shows that, very soon, you will be enjoying a host of rewards.

Helpful Audience!

☺ *I was delivering an address as chief guest at a function in Pune, when the electricity in that building failed. The organizers managed to start the stand-by power supply system and succeeded in illuminating the hall.*

As I stood up again, I muttered to myself, "Now, where was I?"

Someone in the audience loudly shouted, "Right at the end!"

Novelty!

☺ *Two men were traveling in a city bus and were talking.*

"What do you do for living?" asked one.

"I stamp letters at the post office."

"That must be a boring job."

"Boring? Never! We get to stamp a different date everyday!"

Sense of Humor!

☺ *The aging consultant had appointed a young and cute secretary. One day he asked her, "Dear Kavita, what is it that you like most in me, my looks or my intellect?"*

The young lady thought for a second and replied, "Your sense of Humor sir, sense of Humor!"

Pay-slip and Sherlock Holmes!

☺ *Packing department supervisor on pay day: "This month my pay-slip has more deductions than any Sherlock Holmes story!"*

A very common question asked is: "Can I use SDH when the topic of discussion is a multi-crore issue or when the subject under debate involves the lives of thousands of people?"

The answer is an emphatic "yes," with a proviso that you should understand one important difference. Self-directed Humor does not suggest that you should at anytime take your work or responsibilities lightly; it only suggests that there is no need to take yourself seriously. You are directed to take your obligations with utmost importance. Self-directed Humor is useful even when you are in the midst of an emergency: it keeps your vanity in control, it builds affinity with the people around you and helps you in gaining the proper approach to the issue at hand.

Ronald Reagan

☺ *When Ronald Reagan was US President, an American plane attacked two Libyan jets. It was midnight and the President was fast asleep. The President's staff thought it unnecessary to awaken the President and this caused a big commotion the next day. When Reagan came to know the developments,* he declared, "I've made strict rules to be followed by all the staff members. From now on, whatever may happen, they should see that I'm awakened irrespective of the time of the day, even if I am in a cabinet meeting!"

☺ The US President Ronald Reagan was severely censured by many because he ordered the production of B-1 bombers to augment the striking capability of US Air Force.

His reaction to this censure was, "I've been getting some flak about ordering the production of the B-1. How could I know that it was an airplane? I thought it was a vitamin for the troops!"

☺ In 1981, there was an attempt to assassinate Ronald Reagan, who was wounded by a gunshot. When he regained consciousness, one of his senior staff reported to him, "You'll be happy to know that the government is running normally."

Immediately Reagan quipped, "What makes you think I'd be happy about that?"

Financial Advisor

☺ The MD of an Indian company which produced health care equipment had the misfortune to see his company sink deeper and deeper into the red for three consecutive years.

He called his finance director and asked whether anything would get him out of the mess he was in. The finance director thought for a long time and said, "Yes, death would help!"

Price of Promotion

☺ A design engineer in a pump-making company was promoted. He was congratulated by many of his colleagues. But the

*designer gave the following response, "They might have looked
at someone else's progress report. Anyway, now I have to act
as if I know what I'm doing!"*

Self-directed Humor can be used to make meetings,
which form an essential part of business, effective. Usually
these meetings fail to deliver what they are expected to
because participants tend to dwell on irrelevant matters;
they revel in excessive mudslinging or lose interest in doing
what they are supposed to do. It can rejuvenate the
participants, can bring in fresh air to the tense atmosphere,
and set the wheels of the agenda rolling.

You can make a rule for yourself: before laughing at
anyone else (either present or not present at the meeting),
you will laugh at yourself first. This simple formula will
enable you to score over your tormentors in almost every
issue. By being the first to laugh at yourself, you disarm
your opponents who want to ridicule you. You spring a
surprise on them by taking the initiative at poking fun at
yourself. This technique can be very handy whether you are
talking for yourself, or for your team, or for your company.

Another major benefit of this approach is that SDH, like
other forms of Humor, is contagious. By and by, your example will be emulated by other participants in the meeting;
the discussions tend to become more objective. There will
be less heat and more light in the discussions.

Self-directed Humor finds useful application when you
are required to criticize someone. It acts like a sugar coating
on a bitter pill. The amusement that Humor causes smoothens
the sharpness of the censure. Further, as you include yourself
among the criticized, the offence is silenced effectively.
In such a case the outcome would generally be an

enthusiastic promise to correct the mistake or to undo the side effects.

Advantages of Being Slow!

☺ *My friend, Srinivas Vaidya, who was the senior branch manager of a scheduled bank in Mumbai shares the following experience: "One day, a middle-aged man came along with his son to open a joint savings account at the bank. That day the counter was manned by a substitute clerk as the regular person was on leave. The former was known for his slowness and he took a long time to complete the formalities. He found that the boy's age was only 17.5 years old and thus as per the rules was not eligible to open an account. The clerk rejected the application thereby sending the customer into a rage. The customer went to the branch manager and complained how two hours of his time had been wasted by the clerk.*

The branch manager patiently listened to the irate client, then called the clerk and said, "Mr Kamath, you can open their joint savings account. By the time we complete our formalities the boy would have completed 18 years of age. So you need not have any fears!"

Self-directed Humor has been very effectively used in intergroup exchanges. For instance, someone narrates a humorous event which makes his own group appear foolish, momentarily. He and his group members laugh; they are laughing at themselves. It has been observed that such jokes and this type of laughter help in improving the unity and solidarity of the group. Once again, it is very important to see that the self-deprecation is within limits. Carrying it too far may result in undesirable repercussions.

Getting Organised

☺ A small-scale industrialist in Bangalore wanted a bank loan so he could buy a diesel generating set for his plant to counter the erratic power supply of the state. The bank manager asked him to fill in the prescribed application form, to provide a copy of the resolution of the board of directors, and a write-up detailing the purpose of the loan and how it would be repaid. The loan was sanctioned within three days.

A year later the same industrialist wanted to buy some computers and allied equipment. He approached the bank for another loan and explained how the improved financial performance of his company since the installation of the diesel generator has encouraged his company to invest more in capital equipment. The bank manager directed the industrialist to the assistant manager (loans), who in turn directed him to the case worker. The case worker then asked the applicant to give his application form to his assistant. The assistant said he required four weeks to scrutinize the application as there were many earlier applications to be dealt with.

The industrialist was surprised at the change in situation at the bank. He went back to the manager and asked him why the service level had deteriorated. The manager smiled and replied, "You got the earlier loan before we got ourselves organized to serve the customer!"

Corruption

☺ US President George Bush, former British Prime Minister Tony Blair, and the Indian Prime Minister Manmohan Singh met together to discuss the common pressing problems of their respective countries.

*They came to a unanimous agreement that corruption
was the worst common menace and decided to seek divine help
in eliminating it. So, all the three leaders went to meet God.*

*The American President said, "Dear God, I have taken
so many steps to eradicate corruption; when is it going to
disappear from the face of my country?"*

God said, "At this rate, it will take 50 years from now."

*The President felt depressed and dejected that he would
not be alive to see the end of corruption in his country.*

*Next in line was Tony Blair who asked God the same
question about his country. The reply God gave was that it
will take 100 years. Blair was also in tears as he would not
be alive to see the elimination of corruption in his country
either.*

*When it was Manmohan Singh's turn, he too posed the
same question. This time it was the Almighty God who
broke into tears and started crying bitterly. With a choking
voice God said, "I'm not sure whether corruption in India
will end during MY lifetime!"*

Self-directed Humor is the mark of a person's intellectual
superiority and mental well-being. When you can laugh at
yourself you are far more likely to experience cordial
relationships with the people around you. Your wife, your
children, your close friends, your assistants, and your peers
will find themselves emulating you because SDH is highly
infectious. This works wonders because your group, once
hitched on to SDH, will continue to be on the lookout for
opportunities to display it. As a result, the group's
psychological flexibility and maturity will improve. Very
soon your team will be more closely knit and in a position
to take up greater challenges.

Checked and Striped!

☺ *I accompanied my assistant design manager to the Pune airport as she was to fly to Indore on office work. She was flying by a private airline. When she tried to check in the official at the counter told her that because she has taken advantage of a certain discount in the tariff she would not be allowed any checked baggage. My assistant was not perturbed. She calmly said, "Mine is not checked, it is striped. Will you allow it?"*

Specialists

☺ *A teacher wanted to test the memory power of her students from the fourth standard. She read out the story of the elephant and the five blind men to the children and they seemed to enjoy the story. Later she asked the children: "The five men inspected the animal, one said that it was like a wall; another said it was like a column; the third said it resembled a huge fan; the other two said it was like a rope and sword respectively. Now, who will tell me, what kind of people were they?"*

Gopi jumped to his feet and shouted, "Specialists, Miss, they were all specialists!"

Glad to be Home

☺ *A sixth standard student went to his annual school picnic with great enthusiasm. But it appears that his expectations of an enjoyable picnic didn't match the actual experience. A big red ant bit him; he fell into a ditch while trying to catch a butterfly; a monkey snatched away his sandwich and mocked at him from the safety of a high tree branch; and the little girl sitting next to him, pulled his hair. In addition, the hot sun was scorching. When the boy came home in the evening he was exhausted and depressed. His mother was curious to know whether he had enjoyed the picnic. The boy said, "I am so glad that I am back home that I am glad I went!"*

Plumbing

☺ *A teacher asked her class to solve a problem involving water tanks of different sizes, leaky taps, leakage rates, etc. While correcting their work she came across one notebook in which just an eight digit number had been written as the answer. It appeared to have no relevance to the problem so she asked the concerned student to explain. The boy said, "Whenever a tap leaks in our house, we call the plumber and I have written down his telephone number!"*

A vast majority of politicians, speakers, and writers have mastered this skill of SDH; they have placed before us a myriad masterpieces for our guidance. Every businessman who desires to hone his SDH skill is advised to study them. A few examples are given below.

Agatha Christie

☺ *"I married an archaeologist because the older I grow, the more he appreciates me!"*

Kota Shivarama Karanth

☺ *Kota Shivarama Karanth, the great Kannada novelist, folk-dance researcher, educationist, social reformer, and intellectual of the first order has narrated the following experience:*

"I used to teach Hindi language to the students of fourth and fifth standards at Canara High School. By doing this I thought I was doing a great service to our country. But the poor students found learning Hindi to be a great strain. They spoke Konkani at home, Tulu with the general public, and were required to learn Kannada and English at school. As they were already heavily encumbered, my patriotic enthusiasm only added to their strain. So it was not surprising that they saw a villain in me. Instead of calling me "Hindi teacher" they would call me "Handee teacher!" (Handee in Kannada means Pig.) I was so foolish that I never understood the problems of the poor students till their attendance dropped to zero."

Naa Kasturi

☺ *Kasturi was the principal of the DRM government college, Davanagere, Karnataka. Once when Kasturi was at the college, thieves broke into his house and rifled through his belongings. When this news reached Kasturi, the police accompanied him to his house. The police inspector asked Kasturi to lodge a complaint giving the details of the damage caused and goods stolen. But Kasturi refused to lodge any complaint. He said, "It would be impossible for the police to restore what I have lost."*

The inspector disagreed with Kasturi and assured him that the success rate of his staff in catching thieves was very high. Kasturi said, "Mr Inspector, you haven't understood me. Even if you catch the thieves, what I have lost is lost forever!"

"How could that be?" asked the Inspector.

"Well, the thieves have walked away with my well-guarded secret; the secret is that I don't have anything worth stealing. Now this secret would be published. What can you do about it?"

President Reagan

☺ *"There are advantages to being elected President; the day after being sworn in I had my poor school grades classified as top secret!"*

President Clinton (at Jaipur)

☺ *"The palace monkeys first took interest in me, snatched away my garlands, and flowers. After the deflowering, they promptly lost all interest in me."*

Mark Twain

☺ *"I once arrived at Memphis town in the afternoon. I had several hours to spend before dinner and my evening lecture. So I stopped at the general store and said to the owner, 'Good afternoon, friend; is there any entertainment here tonight that would amuse a stranger?'*

The storekeeper wiped his hands on his apron, looked thoughtful and said, 'I expect there's going to be some feller Twain giving a lecture. I think this Twain has no idea of the fellers here. Anyway I've been selling eggs and tomatoes all day!'"

Sir Walter Scott

☺ *"My servant is a great admirer of my novels. He says: 'Your books are really great! They are so useful to me, you know. Every night I needn't struggle to get sleep. The moment I open any of them, I'm already asleep!'"*

George Bernard Shaw

☺ *A reporter once said to Shaw: "You've a marvelous gift for oratory; how did you develop it?"*

Shaw replied, "I learnt to speak as children learn to skate or cycle, by doggedly making a fool of myself until I got used to it!"

Abraham Lincoln

☺ *Abraham Lincoln once sent an important message through his messenger to his secretary of war, Edwin Stanton, who was far away. Stanton though very capable didn't always agree with Lincoln. The former was also often very blunt and stubborn. When he received Lincoln's message he was not in the best of moods. The message irritated him and he shouted out, "President Lincoln is a fool!"*

The messenger who was a witness to this scene reported it to Lincoln and waited to hear Lincoln rebuke Stanton in the choicest words. He was in for a big disappointment; Lincoln smiled and only said, "Probably Stanton is right!"

Winston Churchill

☺ *Churchill was to deliver a speech at a function. He was holding a piece of paper when he spoke. The person sitting* next to Churchill on the rostrum had observed that what Churchill held in his hand was an old shopping list and did not contain any notes for the speech.

After the speech, the person was curious to know how the shopping list helped Churchill in making the speech. Churchill replied, "I know it was an old shopping list. I held the piece of paper so that it gave confidence to the audience."

Soviet Humor

☺ Once a Russian citizen gate-crashed the Kremlin, into the most guarded building. He was shouting continuously, "Khruschev is a great fool, Khruschev is a great fool!"

The Russian was arrested and was sentenced to 23 years of rigorous imprisonment in a Siberian prison.

When Khruschev narrated this incident to the US President John F. Kennedy, the President asked, "Why 23 years?"

Khruschev replied, "Three years for insulting the First Secretary of the Communist Party and 20 years for revealing a state secret!"

Mahatma Gandhi

☺ When Mahatma Gandhi visited England for the Round Table Conference he had an appointment with the British king. Gandhiji went to meet the king in his normal dress: a half dhoti covering the body from the waist to the knees and a cotton shawl.

When Gandhiji came out of the meeting, press reporters were eager to know if Gandhiji was embarrassed with his strange dress when he met the king. Gandhiji replied, "Why *should I be embarrassed? Eighty percent of my countrymen dress like me. The king wore a dress which would have clothed two people easily. So the average worked out to a very respectable amount!"*

Speech Making!

☺ *William Lyon Phelps, Yale University professor and popular lecturer said, "Everytime I accept an invitation to speak, I really make four speeches but I get credit only for one-fourth of these speeches. First is the speech I prepare in advance; that is pretty good. Second is the speech I actually make at the venue; third is the speech I make on my way home; and fourth is the speech the newspapers report next morning, which bears no relation to any of the others!"*

Theodore Roosevelt

☺ *Roosevelt was one of the very famous US Presidents. Before becoming the President he had been an attorney. In those days he used to be very heavily built. On one occassion he had been to a nearby town to meet a client and was returning to New York. In those days the railways were owned by private companies and there used to be a provision that the trains could be requested to stop by any group of passengers for being picked up. Roosevelt had sent a message for the train to stop to pick up a large party. The train stopped and when only Roosevelt got in, the conductor asked, "Where is your large party?"*

Roosevelt, pointing towards his huge anatomy, replied, "I am that large party!"

Benjamin Franklin

☺ *Franklin recorded the following experience in his auto-biography and would narrate it in his speeches. He was once invited for a conference by a literary society in Paris. Franklin did not know French well, but he wanted to be polite and well behaved in that conference and so decided that whenever his hostess Mme De Boufflers, would applaud, he would follow suit. After the meeting, Franklin's little grandson said to him, "But, grandpa, why were you applauding so loudly, louder than all others when the speakers were saying good about you?"*

SDH for Anyone

The following anecdotes and stories can provide you with ready material for launching your SDH in your environment. It may be necessary that you be required to prepare a light introduction so that there is no abruptness in your narrative. This introduction serves the purpose of bringing in the relevance of what you are going to say to your situation and group. You may also need to select the anecdote most suitable for the occasion. You are also welcome to use any of the examples given earlier, with the necessary adaptation.

The Computer Wizard and the Genie

☺ *A computer programmer was walking along the beach when he found a brass lamp. When he rubbed the lamp, a genie appeared and said, "I'm the most powerful genie in the world. I can grant you any wish you want, but only one wish."*

The programmer pulled out a map of Kashmir and said, "I'd like to see lasting peace among the people of India and Pakistan after a mutually satisfying agreement over the issue of Kashmir."

The genie replied, "That's not easy, these people have hated each other for decades. I can do just about anything, but this is beyond my limits."

The programmer then said, "Well, I'm a software programmer. My services are sought after by many multinational companies. Make all my clients satisfied with my programs and let them ask for only sensible changes."

The genie replied, "What you are asking for is even more difficult. Ok, let me see that Kashmir map again!"

(You can adapt this story to suit your profession instead of using computer programming as a profession.)

Therapy

☺ *"My therapist told me that the way to achieve inner peace was to finish what I start. So far today, I have finished two bags of chips and a black forest cake. I feel better already!"*

Screw-Loose Speaker

☺ *A speaker was facing some difficulty with the sound system. Finally, the repair man handed him a note which said, "We've found what the trouble is. There is a loose screw in the speaker!"*

(You can narrate this as though you were the speaker.)

I'm a Great Scientist!

☺ *"It took Sir William Ramsay 16 years to discover Helium; the Curies took 30 years to discover Radium. But yet, I can, in 10 minutes, produce Tedium."*

Sure and Unsure

☺ *Till recently, I considered myself as something of a philosopher and never missed an opportunity to give bits of sage advice to my grandchildren.*

One day I was telling my granddaughter, Ketaki, "Remember, it's the fools who are certain; the wise are somewhat unsure always."

"Are you sure, Baba?" she asked.

"Yes, my dear lady. I'm absolutely certain."

Hearing me she started laughing loudly. I couldn't understand her laughter initially. After a few seconds, I laughed at my own foolishness."

Albert Einstein

☺ *The Einsteins were being interviewed on the occasion of their golden wedding anniversary. A reporter asked Albert, "What's the secret behind your long, successful marriage?"*

Einstein replied, "When we got married, we made a pact. All the big decisions would be made by me; my wife would decide all others. And we have kept to it all these 50 years. That, I think, is the secret of our successful marriage."

He then paused and added, "The strange thing is that in these 50 years there hasn't yet been a big decision!"

No Leave Please!

☺ *I had put in about 10 years of service at my job and had been elevated to the post of a divisional head. After my promotion, I did not feel like taking privilege leave. Year after year my leave would accumulate and then lapse beyond the limit of 60 days. A colleague of mine asked me, "You don't take privilege leave! Why? Can your division not manage for two weeks without you?"*

"There's no doubt that the division can run without me. But I don't want anyone to discover this possibility!"

Revenge

☺ *I once had car trouble on the outskirts of my city. I asked a truck driver, who happened to be proceeding in my direction, to help tow my car to the nearest garage.*

On the way my wife kept protesting that the amount charged by the truck driver to do the job was too high. She said, "It's scandalous to charge us Rs 1,000 for towing the car only 20 km."

I consoled her saying, "Never mind, dear; I'm having my revenge on that fellow. I've got the brakes on!"

My Embarrassing Experience

☺ *I was once at Frankfurt Airport as a transit passenger. I had about two hours of time to spend before embarking on the flight to New York. I bought a small packet of biscuits and sat down to read a magazine. Shortly, I heard a swishing sound which attracted my attention and I looked up from behind my magazine. A well-dressed young lady was helping herself to my biscuits. I thought that she was probably hungry and therefore didn't want to object. I also helped myself to a couple of them and returned to my reading. A few minutes passed and I heard more swishing sounds. The lady was eating one biscuit after another rather nonchalantly and soon the packet was empty. Holding the last biscuit the woman had the temerity to break it into two and offer me one half. She ate the other half and left her seat with a smile on her face. I was positively angry at the rudeness of the woman. Just then my flight was announced and I opened my briefcase to get my transit card. To my embarrassment, there I saw my unopened pack of biscuits! My assumptions had made an ass of me!*

Deserving Heaven

☺ *A clergyman and a taxi driver who happened to die on the same day traveled to the Gates of Heaven. The Lord met them at the steps and pronounced his decision: "Take the clergyman to Hell and the taxi driver to Heaven." This was totally shocking to the clergyman. He appealed to the Lord, "There's some error; it's I who deserve Heaven."*

But the Lord replied, "There can be no mistakes in my judgment. Can you recall how you put so many people who came to church to pray to me to sleep by your sermons? Do you think that that was the way to serve me? On the other hand, the taxi driver, whenever he drove, would make his passengers sit up and pray for their safety with utmost humility."

(You are advised to alter the clergyman's profession to yours with suitable minor changes in the contents to make the story relevant and logical.)

Conclusion

Laughing at yourself in the midst of others is a mark of your maturity and strength. It makes the people around you relaxed and helps them feel familiar with you. Immediate rapport is built and your words carry more weight. This technique is the easiest, safest, and most effective form of Humor. Always make it a rule to laugh at yourself before laughing at others. By this simple step your friends will become closer, strangers become friends, and enemies think of joining hands with you. Self-deprecating Humor easily spreads from one person to the other, and it can find application in any situation.

Chapter 5

Winning People Over to
Your Point of View

"Laughter removes the burden of seriousness from the problem, and often times it's that very serious attitude that is the problem itself!"
—Bob Basso

Communicating is the most important activity in any business. According to available statistics, the senior-most managers spend about 94 percent of their working hours in communicating or in preparing themselves for communicating. Those in middle management devote 80 percent of their time and the ones lower in the hierarchy, about 70 percent. Meetings account for 53 percent of communicating time, telephonic conversations take up 16 percent, written communications occupy 25 percent, and the remaining time is spent on preparations. Everyone in the company is a communicator; each of us has messages for someone or the other. All these communications seem to have one sole purpose and that is to persuade others. Your message to people is futile unless you succeed in making them listen to you and bear it in mind. Similarly, if you are sending out a written communication, you have to ensure that the receiver is enticed to read it and remember its contents. An intelligent blending of Humor into your communications is the smartest method of bolstering your expertise in communicating. Humor is a very powerful device through which you can create affinity, attract attention, entertain people, help them remember your message, and put them into a mood very favorable to your influence.

The Speaker and the Listener

At first sight it looks as though you as the speaker have all the advantages and, in theory, you should find it easy to influence the audience. You are positioned on a dais and stand under a spotlight. You are the only one in the hall to have a lectern and a microphone. The audience is seated facing you in complete attention toward you. But everything is not in your favor. To start with, you suffer from a strong minority disadvantage because you have to single-handedly face the audience. Next, you are likely to have butterflies in your stomach in the initial stages. In addition, there generally is an antagonistic atmosphere between the audience and you in the beginning. The latter is very likely to have strong doubts about your competence and could be annoyed at the thought of you exploiting them. Unless you already have well-established credentials, they tend to harbor some hostility. They are more likely to ignore you and your words; they may even engage themselves in fault-finding in each of your statements and finally in your overall message. So, it is of paramount importance that you establish a rapport with the audience right from the beginning of your talk. This will encourage most of your audience to like you and accept what you say. There could be some in the audience who disagree with what you say, but your rapport-building efforts can make them listen to you with attention. Let me explain in detail the benefits you can enjoy from the proper use of Humor.

Humor Achieves Affinity

When you as a speaker use Humor, you overcome your initial nervousness. Humor demands that you be your natural self and this makes you even more self-assured. While using Humor, you are tacitly declaring to the audience that you're one with them and that you have a clear grasp of the facts relating to them and their problems. You're also hinting that you have something useful to offer to them. This will build up a certain degree of familiarity between you and your listeners. Some of the audience may begin to respect you and your words. Your status or the power you wield will be of little use while dealing with the audience. Humor can deliver more favorable results than your status and authority. In fact, it is sometimes likely that your status and authority may work against you when you are trying to build a rapport. Some successful speakers have used the following jokes to break ice with their audiences. You may build your own collection of similar Humor lines. A few examples are given below.

☺ *"I never give advice to others because they feel obliged to repay me!"*

—Pat Williams

☺ *"In my first job I was told by my employer, "I know, that you can't afford to get married on the money that I'm paying you, young man. Some day you will thank me for it!"*

—Pat Williams

☺ *"I was never a 'Yes' man. When my boss said 'No,' I too would say 'no'!"*

—Pat Williams

☺ *"Right now, I am learning how to deal with stress, while my boss is attending a seminar to learn how to create it!"*

☺ *"The advantage of having a secretary to take minutes at the meeting is great; there would be at least one person who's giving attention to what is being said!"*

—Pat Williams

☺ *"My son is a born executive; he's only five, but already he takes two and a half hours for lunch!"*

—Pat Williams

☺ *"There are some people who do things because they have been done earlier; there are others who do things because they have not been done before!"*

Spicing your talk with Humor entertains your audience and all listeners love to be entertained. In turn, they start taking a liking towards you; not only that, they exchange silent communications among themselves to reassure themselves that they are together in enjoying your Humor.

Humor Gets Attention

Everyone wants to laugh; laughing without reason is not generally accepted in our society. You might have observed crowds in trade fairs and exhibitions thronging the stalls which display funny things like a lottery game, a magic show, or some unusual acrobatic feat, etc. At conferences and seminars, delegates who form small groups and laugh are the centers of attraction for other visitors. Creating laughter is the most common way of making people happy and relaxed.

If you think the topic is so important that there is no scope for Humor in your presentation, you would be making a cardinal mistake. The fact that your message is very important makes it imperative that you ensure it gets everyone's attention.

Prompt Response!

☺ *A young girl was studying at university far away from her parents' place. She was not regular in writing to her parents about her welfare, even though they wrote regularly. The girl's grandmother assured the parents that she would arrange to receive a letter from the college girl within a week, and she did receive it. There was a pretty longish letter from the college girl which had this postscript: "Dear Grandma, you had written that you had enclosed a cheque for Rs 2,000. But it was not there. I'm waiting for your next letter."*

Distracting Listeners

☺ *There is a story of how the famous defense lawyer Clarence Darrow won a court case through the ingenious use of practical Humor. The case hearing was almost over; the prosecutor stood up to present his concluding argument. During this time Darrow lit a cigar and started smoking in silence. There was nothing unusual about it except that the defense lawyer made it a point not to make use of the ashtray. In fact, he took special care not to flick the cigar at all lest the ash would drop down. As the ash grew in length, everyone in the court (especially the jurors), was keen to see when the ash would fall. The prosecutor went on arguing, but the jurors kept watching Darrow's cigar, especially the lengthening ash part of it. Soon the ash had become so long that it was bound to fall down any moment. By then the jurors had lost track of the prosecutor's contentions and were staring at the cigar. Darrow had secretly provided metallic wire support to his cigar, so that the ash would stay put even when it grew 10 cm long.*

Humor Retains Attention

A friend of mine once invited me to attend a discourse by Swami Chinmayananda. As I happened to be very tired that day, I expressed my deep regret and explained the reason for my inability to attend the talk. My friend laughed loudly and said that I could get total rest while listening to Swamiji's talk. My friend is not alone in believing that listening is a totally passive, restful activity. It is not. When we listen, our body and brain are quite active. We have to hear every word; we have to be alert and focus all our attention on the speaker. We have to understand what is said, scrutinize every statement, decide which is believable and which is not, and filter in all the statements for acceptance on their individual merit. Even when we have gained very useful knowledge, the activities we are required to put in amount to hard and studious work, and this surely saps our energy and causes fatigue, over time. If the speaker does not provide us any respite, we involuntarily seek our own ways of taking a brief diversion: we may leave the speaker to his/her own means and think about the shopping we have to do with the family that evening, or think about fixing a bridge session at home during the coming weekend.

As a shrewd speaker, you should therefore plan to provide the interludes needed to rejuvenate your listeners and to invigorate them. These interludes need not be very long; a good quotation, a witty observation, or an appropriate anecdote will help in retaining the attention of your audience. Here are some examples.

Telling the Truth

☺ *Gene Perret, the comic writer for Bob Hope, in one of his talk shows said, "Sometimes I find it so difficult to tell the truth. Truth hurts people a great deal. I once visited a friend and his daughter who had delivered a baby boy a month earlier showed me the baby and asked me whether the baby was not very, very pretty. I had not seen an uglier baby so far. I was in a fix. Finally I blurted out, 'The baby is just like its Pa!'"*

Canine Interest!

☺ *A speaker was addressing the delegates at a seminar in a city in Gujarat, a few days after the state had suffered from earthquakes. During the course of his talk, he digressed from the topic and said that some seismologists had advanced a new theory on how pet animals could sense earthquakes in advance. The seismologists recommended that people keenly observe the behavior of their pets so they can be forewarned of any impending quake and rush to safety. The speaker went on to say that had he observed his two pet Great Danes on that day a bit more closely, he could have predicted the disaster two hours in advance. On that day his dogs took away his Maruti 800 to Rajkot!*

Humor Makes Things Easy to Understand

The analogy of a piece of Humor to the situation being discussed makes it easy for the listeners to understand what is being said. The humorous story is listened to with rapt attention and hence the subject matter is driven home with only a brief explanation. Understanding the principles behind the joke can help the listener grasp your point of view clearly.

That's not my Dog!

☺ *In 1984, Senator Glenn was criticizing Ronald Reagan in his presidential campaign. Glenn recalled an old story: "An old man was standing inside a fenced building complex. A visitor came to the gate and tried to enter. Soon a full-grown German Shepard came running toward the gate. The visitor asked the old man, 'Does your dog bite?'*

The old man said, 'No.'

On hearing this the visitor confidently opened the gate and entered. To his horror, the dog pounced on him and sank his teeth into his calf muscle. Naturally, the visitor was enraged and berated old man for lying. The old man only said, 'That's not my dog!'"

After narrating this story, the Senator went on to state that Reagan was not accepting that federal deficit was his folly. "Reagan says it's not his dog which is biting us!"

☺ *The spare parts division of a company had fared poorly in three consecutive quarters. The divisional manager called his people together to give them a pep talk and to have a brainstorming session to list the possible solutions to the various problems being faced. He made it clear that if things didn't improve it was quite likely that the division would have to be closed down and all the needs of the company would have to be met through outsourcing. This meant compulsory premature retirement to many. Then he made a very succinct point, "I'm not saying that you should save your jobs; I'm saying that you should save MY job!"*

There was no need to further explain the gravity of the situation.

Humor Makes Points Memorable

A doctor friend of mine tells me that a number of his elderly patients seek his help because they feel very depressed. One of his prescriptions to them is, "try recapturing your past." When the patients do try to do this, they are in for a very pleasant surprise. They think of the places where they were happy when young, the specific incidents which made them happy, the persons involved, the weather conditions at the time, the words spoken, the activities in which they indulged, and many more graphic details of all those happy moments. Most of them wondered how they could remember all those minute details even after so many years.

The human memory is like that. We remember the good things we hear, the joy we experience, the excitement we feel, for a very long time. It is this phenomenon which allows your message to remain fresh in the memory of your listeners for a long time; because your message and the Humor you used in your talk gives them a pleasant experience. As you had taken special care to link Humor and your message appropriately, your listeners are very likely to retain your point.

George Schultz

☺ *Former US Secretary of State, George Schultz, whenever he was out of the capital, used to include a joke in every cable he sent to President Ronald Reagan. When Schultz returned to Washington, he would know that his message had got through if the President said, "That was a great joke, George!"*

They shouldn't Hear You!

☺ *A sales engineer was negotiating to secure a big order from one of his prospective clients, but there was a great deal of delay. The client was changing his requirements very frequently and was also asking for a stringent warranty. The chances of getting the order were improving, but at a snail's pace.*

The sales manager was furious; he started criticizing the sales engineer very sarcastically. The sales engineer interrupted his boss midway and said, "Sir, please wait a moment."

He pulled out his wallet, took out two photographs from it and stuffed them into his briefcase. Then he said, "Sir, I have a wife and two children, and I didn't want them to hear this kind of language. Okay, you can now continue!"

The boss realized that he had allowed himself to be overcome by his anger and apologized. He also made it a point not to berate his deputy in future.

Humor Relieves Stress

Stress is very common whenever you decide to speak in public. Meetings are notorious for taking place in a tense atmosphere right from beginning to end. Many items in the agenda of the meeting, either inadvertently or on purpose, point an accusing finger at someone or the other. A meeting scheduled to discuss the delays in the execution of orders on hand is sure to create tension when the marketing managers, design engineers, and the production supervisors exchange accusations and compete in a fault-finding game. It would not surprise anyone if the scheduled duration of the meeting gets over and nothing substantial is achieved. In such situations, a humorous approach helps you make people identify the problems and engage themselves in finding solutions, not scapegoats.

I'm the One at Fault!

☺ *A designer and a production engineer started arguing over some changes in the design of a component. Slowly, they both became more angry; their quarrel attracted the attention and curiousity of the other employees who stopped their work to see who would be the winner. Someone ran up to the manager to inform him about what was happening. The manager called both deputies to his office, listened to their contentions, and said, "Look here boys, both of you, now calm down. Neither of you is at fault… I'm the one who is at fault here! Am I not the one who hired both of you? Now, can you both go ahead and find a solution to the problem by putting your heads together, before the end of this shift?"*

Brian Close

☺ *The legendary Yorkshire cricketer, Brian Close, known for his limitless toughness on the field, was a close-in fielder in a closely contested match. The batsman pulled the ball savagely and the ball hit Close, nastily on his cheek. The ball then jumped upward to be caught by a slip fielder. Brian's colleagues were happy that the batsman was out, but were worried about their teammate's injury. Luckily for Brian it was not a serious injury and they were all relieved. One player did wonder what would have happened had the ball hit Brian on the nose.*

Brian laughed and said, "In that case the blighter would have been caught at cover!"

Everyone laughed and the tension in the air got cleared.

Humor can Dismiss Hostility

Humor creates laughter. One cannot laugh and hate simultaneously. With laughter there is bound to be a dip in the hatred. Humor resembles Judo, in which the expert employs quick movements and leverage to overpower the opponent, using the opponent's heavier body weight or greater momentum against him.

Anti-God Society

☺ *Gandhiji was once approached by a youth who said to him, "I'm an atheist. I'm organizing an anti-God society. I request you to address our gathering this Saturday evening."*

Gandhiji smiled and said, "Young man, I'm amazed at your approach. You've declared that you don't believe that God exists. Then why are you craving to fight against Him, who according to you does not at all exist? Where, then, is the need for your anti-God society?"

Who Started the Joke?

☺ *A youth who had a degree in Information Technology was facing his first job interview. The personnel manager asked him, "In case you are selected, what emoluments would you expect?"*

"Anywhere above Rs 200,000 per month depending on the fringe benefits."

"How do you like," asked the personnel manager, "a salary package of four weeks of privilege leave, three weeks of casual leave, four weeks of fully paid sick leave, full coverage of medical expenses, three weeks paid vacation, a 30 percent superannuation fund, and a company car, mostly an Audi?"

The candidate was taken aback at this unbelievable offer and asked with excitement, "Are you joking or what?"

"Exactly," said the personnel manager. "But you were the first to start it, I only continued it!"

Donning a Moustache

☺ A company had invited applications for the post of a senior manager in their finance division. The selection committee interviewed the short-listed candidates and had finalized one when they received an application from a lady candidate with a highly impressive resume. She was called in for an interview. At the end of the interview, the committee members felt that they should stick with their earlier choice. The leader said to the lady: "Well, Mrs Iyer, we find you otherwise suitable, but we need a man for this job. All the existing staff in this division are males."

But the lady was not the least put down. She smiled and said, "That's no problem for me. I can attend office in full suit and tie. I can take instructions like married men. I can act tough while negotiating. But don't ask me to don a moustache!"

The lady used Humor very cleverly, displaying her adaptability, composure, courage, and ingenuity. Needless to say she was selected.

Humor is Goal-Oriented

Most people are unaware of the fact that Humor gets the desired results, even when all other methods fail. This marvel has been experienced particularly when disputes, discords, and controversies have to be resolved. In these situations it is common for people to lose sight of reason and logic as they are blinded by self-conceit and vanity. The real problems are neglected and non-existent problems engage them. Humor helps to clear the air and bring back objectivity.

Business and Jugglery

☺ *The central minister for industries was addressing a conference of small-scale industrialists in Bangalore. In his address, the minister referred to a news report of an Indian juggler who had created a Guinness record by crossing the Grand Canyon riding a bicycle on a tight wire rope. The minister exhorted the industrialists to emulate the juggler and face the challenges of the global market.*

One industrialist stood up and submitted to the minister, "I congratulate the juggler on his record-breaking success. But I would like to draw the attention of our honorable minister and his officers to the fact that the odds against us in running our businesses are more formidable. The juggler had many factors in his favor: he was not required to make any under-the-table payments; he was not harassed by unscheduled power cuts. Moreover, no one was working on the wire rope with a power hacksaw!"

This analogy had everyone in splits; the minister too couldn't help laughing. More importantly, the appeal had registered in his mind and in his reply he expressed concern

FIGURE 7
Meetings! Meetings!

for the small-scale industrialists and assured them that he would initiate steps to mitigate the problems they faced.

Received All Dues!

☺ *The accounts manager of a small-scale engineering company had repeatedly, though unsuccessfully, tried to collect arrears from a reputed public sector company. Finally, he rang up the chief finance officer of the company and said, "If we don't receive our overdue payments by tomorrow, we will intimate all your creditors that we have received not only our overdues, but also the dues up to last week!"*

Swami Vivekananda

☺ *In 1897, Swami Vivekananda reached the city of Chicago, in the US, to participate in the Parliament of World Religions as India's representative. He was only obeying an inner voice in undertaking his first ever overseas visit. He had not planned his visit and was ignorant about the exact date and venue of the convention. Guided by his zeal to present the essence of Hinduism, he arrived in Chicago a fortnight earlier. He knew no one in the city and was not sure about how to support himself there. While he was contemplating his next step, an American lady approached him and asked, "Sir, have you arrived here to participate in the forum on world religions?"*

Swamiji replied in the affirmative. The lady asked, "Do you have any acquaintances here?"

Swamiji again replied in the affirmative. Then the lady asked, "Who are they and where do they live? Perhaps I may help you in taking you to them."

Swamiji had a smile on his face and said, "You are all the acquaintances I have here!"

The lady was highly surprised. She was deeply impressed by the directness, simplicity, and calmness of Swamiji. The sense of Humor that Swamiji displayed appealed to her and she invited him to be her personal guest throughout his stay at Chicago.

Humor can Stimulate and Galavanize

Very often Humor produces miraculous results. The logic of Humor can be so powerful that it stimulates people to rise to meteoric heights. It galvanizes the listeners into extraordinary enthusiasm to carry out impossible tasks.

I'll have to Get Shot Again!

☺ *The US President, Ronald Reagan, faced an assassination attempt in 1981. He suffered a gunshot injury, but luckily for him recovered. This attempt on his life earned him unprecedented sympathy and popularity from his countrymen. In early 1983, unemployment in the US reached its peak. The economic conditions were discouraging and the majority of the American people were disenchanted by the performance of the Reagan Government. The President called a meeting of his deputies and while reviewing the situation, said, "I know what we can do. I will have to go and get shot again!"*

These words inspired the governing body as well as all the senators of the Republican party and their followers, to such a degree that things improved. Reagan's popularity grew by such leaps and bounds that he was reelected President in the 1984 elections!

Guessing Lateness

☺ *A production manager was once annoyed by a worker who was never punctual in reporting to duty. The worker happened to be highly skilled in his trade and used to turn out double the output of an average worker, but still the manager wanted to disicipline the fellow and thought up a very clever ploy. He called all the workers including the habitual latecomer and said, "From tomorrow Mr Mali (the name of the habitual latecomer) will be the center of attention. All of you exluding Mr Mali may guess everyday the exact time at which he would report to duty. Mr Mali has to pay Rs 5 to the colleague whose guess is closest to the actual time of his reporting." Very soon, Mr Mali became one of the most punctual workers in the department.*

Conclusion

Communicating is one activity which occupies the majority of time of all business managers. All communications have one real goal: the sender wants to win the receiver over to his viewpoint. Humor, when appropriately used in these communications, helps you in a subtle way to achieve this goal. Humor makes sure that the audience is in a pleasant mood throughout the presentation. It makes people receive your message attentively and remember it longer. The audience is also motivated to take necessary action as per your communications. The Humor you use should be relevant to the topic of your presentation. Displaying Humor is not your goal; it is only an accessory to help you achieve your main goal of getting your message across to your audience. Do not fear that your Humor may not be very successful. Even if it fails, by and by, you will be seen as a more agreeable speaker than those who do not try any Humor at all.

Chapter 6

Getting Laugh after Laugh!

"Time spent in laughing, is time spent with the Gods!"

—Anonymous

What to Avoid (a)

☺ *The vice president of Strategic Business Unit 1 of the company had called an important meeting of his deputies to discuss how a pending high-value order could be bagged. The experience on an earlier occasion with the same customer had not been a happy one. A competitor company had bagged the order by underquoting by just 1 percent of the value. As per the agenda for the meeting, the marketing manager was the first to address the group detailing their latest position and setting the tone for the discussions on the move. He opened his talk saying, "Yesterday, I came across a funny story which may have a moral for us all. There was an old blacksmith in our village who, as he was getting old and weak, found it beyond his strength to attend to all the chores of his shop. So he recruited a young and sturdy youth from the neighboring village. This young man was not known to be sharp-witted but the blacksmith found him suitable. The blacksmith was very particular that his assistant should listen to his instructions carefully and obey his every word. The youth was not encouraged to ask any questions as his master thought that they only wasted time.*

One day the old man took a piece of white hot iron from the forge with a pair of long tongs and held it on the anvil. He ordered the youth, 'Get that sledgehammer over there,' he said, 'and when I nod my head, hit it with all your strength.' With this order the old man nodded his head and the poor youth obeyed the instructions given to him. As a result, the village had to find a new blacksmith!"

> *"Now, coming to the latest position of the tender bid…"*
> *and the marketing manager went on speaking, but no one in*
> *that meeting could understand if the story had, in any way,*
> *added to any of the points the marketing manager was*
> *making. Finally, everyone there came to the conclusion that*
> *it was only an effort on the part of their marketing manager*
> *to create some laughter, even though such an attempt right at*
> *the beginning of the talk was out of place.*

In a similar manner, many speakers are known to start by saying, "Have you heard of this funny thing?" or "You may stop me if you have heard about this story." It would be next to impossible for you to stop them from telling you the story, regardless of the fact that it may be completely irrelevant.

What to Avoid (b)

☺ *In a board meeting, the annual financial statements of a*
company were to be presented for the approval of the board.
I was told that the managing director (MD) who rose to
welcome the members went on to say: "The other day, I tried
a new shampoo for the first time on the recommendations of
a friend of mine. Do you believe it, the shampoo was really
good. So I thought of complimenting the manufacturer by
sending a congratulatory message by e-mail. This was more
than three weeks ago and I had quite forgotten about it till
yesterday, when a large carton was delivered at my house,
when I was away. The box contained a number of free samples
of many varieties of shampoos, soaps, detergents, hair oils,
and toothpastes. My wife was very excited about the whole
thing. It is her idea that now I should write to the Hyundai
Motor Company!"

The two examples just discussed illustrate the single greatest blunder that speakers commit in their enthusiasm to somehow manage to add Humor to their speeches. People from all walks of life suffer from this weakness. Their desire to use Humor is of course laudable, but the manner in which they use it is abominable. At best, that is when the story is really good, it will generate some titters after which the words are forgotten. The joke/story would serve only as a mild interference in the scheduled program. If it bombs, the speaker faces a very embarrassing situation while continuing his talk. The audience on their part would have diverted their focus and attention from the speaker and it would need *Bhageeratha Prayatna* (Herculean efforts) to regain them.

Fortunately, a few precautions can provide freedom from such predicaments. The main reason for most of the speakers falling into this "Humor trap" is that they devote very little time to choose and blend Humor into their talks. Even those who spend weeks and even months preparing their main speech, do not employ more than a passing moment on the selection of their jokes and stories. The latest joke they have heard impresses them so much that they will be tempted to think that the joke will entertain any group, any time, and at any venue. This erroneous view is only a product of haste and ignorance.

The after-effects of such irrelevant Humor are particularly inauspicious. Some speakers are so embarrassed at their failed Humor that they give up the use of Humor altogether. This is analogous to the reader of *Reader's Digest* who, after reading an article highlighting the harmful effects of smoking, gave up the *Reader's Digest*! Such things happen making real life stranger than fiction. The second group of speakers are to be feared even more; they remain undaunted even when their Humor has failed. They continue to use irrelevant Humor at every possible opportunity and generally get away unscathed. But they should also give up hopes to become good speakers capable of winning others to their point of view. As a striking contrast let us study a couple of cases where Humor is effectively harnessed by the speaker to bolster the point he wants to make.

Making it Relevant (a)

☺ *A meeting had been convened by the head of the heavy engines department. All the foremen were called in order to discuss the methods of improving safety in the department. As many people were eager to speak and the available time was fixed, the head called upon all to present their viewpoints briefly and emphasized that brevity made one's point stronger and not weaker. To support this point he narrated the story of Mark Twain.*

"One Sunday, Mark Twain and his family members went to a church. Mr Hawley, the city missionary, was speaking in order to raise funds for the aid of the starved children of Biafra, Africa. Mr Hawley was very eloquent and his speech, moving. Twain was so deeply impressed by the talk that he took out all the $400 he had in his wallet in readiness to place it in the plate which was about to be circulated. But instead of circulating the plate, the missionary went on with his speech. Soon the speech became a boring affair and $300 of the amount found its way back into the wallet. Twain waited for the plate twirling the $100 note in his hand and still the speech continued. Twain could not stand this any longer. He sent the $100 note into his wallet

and pulled out a $10 note instead. But still the plate did not come. After a delay of another hour, when the plate finally came before Twain, he had the vengeful resolve to pinch 10 cents from the plate!"

Making it Relevant (b)

☺ One day I was called by our works manager and was told that the weekly production coordination meetings would henceforth be convened by me. A more senior officer of the company used to convene these meetings earlier and as he was being transferred to another plant that assignment was being given to me. There were some members who were senior to me and they did not take very kindly to being passed up for the job. In addition, the discussions in these meetings used to get stormy and could test the patience and tact of the convener. I was quite aware of these facts. Yet, I wanted to try my best. So, in the very first meeting, I appealed to all the members that it was only their full cooperation that could make the meetings successful. I also made it clear that I was in no way better qualified to become the convener than the fellow who was made the music conductor at the local music club and told them that story.

"The orchestra group had a lot of trouble with their drummer. The musical director had a chat with him pointing out his mistakes, but the drummer's performance hardly improved. Finally the music director said, before the whole group, 'When a musician just cannot handle his instrument, and doesn't improve with help, they take away the instrument and give him two sticks and make him a drummer. And if he can't handle even that, they take away one of the sticks and make him a conductor!'"

I said that I had been made the convener in a similar manner. When the group realized that I had no "stiff upper lip," the members chipped in enthusiastically and the weekly meetings were quite successful for some years.

From these discussions it should now be clear that Humor has to be relevant in order for it to be effective; it should have some clear purpose in the presentation, otherwise it is a nuisance. It should either be there to highlight the point being made, or it should be there to allay doubts the listener, may harbor. It should make the message more memorable. It may be to humanize you in the eyes of your listeners. Generally, the speaker is thought by the audience to be extraordinary; at least, that's what the speaker believes. When you use Humor to humanize yourself, you are trying to shorten the distance between you and them. You are trying to prove that you are just like them. That is humanizing. It can be used as an amusing diversion to rejuvenate the audience. When Humor is used with a specific purpose, the listeners are more ready to enjoy it; and even if Humor fails to create laughter, the presentation will not suffer. How can you expect a better insurance than this?

Pursue Your Own Pattern

I tried to learn golf, as my boss, who is very fond of the game, invited me to join him. He said that golf was not a very difficult game to learn. I saw him teeing off smoothly; his putts were also crisp and clean. I therefore thought that I could pick up the game quite easily too. There is no need for me to discuss here how my overconfidence reached peak

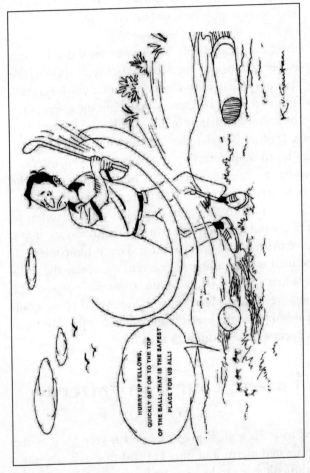

FIGURE 8
Humor and Golf

levels when I thought about the game. My first 10 attempts to tee-off were more like earth-breaking attempts, there being no contact between my iron and the ball. I could hear an ant family, which was being led by their leader, saying, "Fellows, come quick, there is no safety for us in the ground. Hurry up, all of you get on to the ball. That is the safest place for us all!"

Many of my friends have also shared similar experiences. When an expert swings the club for teeing-off, it looks so easy and effortless, and we feel confident of displaying a similar performance. But when novices take up the club and face the ball, everything goes wrong. Our stance, our grip, the focus, the backlift, the follow through, the position of our head, everything. It is the same thing with Humor. A tendency of any novice with Humor is the attempt at being unnatural about everything that is done—the voice, gait, emphasis, etc. If a speaker is able to tell a story that can make others laugh, we think that we can tell the same story equally successfully. Remember, that story suited that speaker's personality. It may not suit you. You have to discover what your Humor style is. Humor can take many forms—jokes, stories, fables, quotes, quips, anecdotes, puns, cartoons, poems, or a mixture of some of these. Identify what makes you laugh most and what you are comfortable reciting. Use your own speech style; do not try to copy the language, voice, or intonation of others. You need to be yourself for maximum effectiveness. You are unique and there is no one like you in the whole world. Exploit this uniqueness fully. Do not lurk behind anybody else's shadow.

The following anecdotes illustrate the unique Humor of three great personalities, viz., Mark Twain, Mahatma Gandhi, and Abraham Lincoln.

Mark Twain (a)

☺ *Mark Twain was once persuaded by his friends in San Francisco to give a lecture on the interesting things he had witnessed in the Hawaiian islands. They assured him that they would laugh heartily at strategic points among the audience, so that an encouraging response to his talk could be definitely managed. But little did they know that Twain never needed artificial support. He started off his talk saying, "Julius Caesar is dead; Shakespeare is dead; Napoleon is dead; Abraham Lincoln is dead; and I am far from well myself." These words had the audience rolling in laughter. As the talk continued, the peals of laughter continued growing.*

Mark Twain (b)

☺ *Mark Twain reached a small town one afternoon during his lecturing days and went to a chemist's shop nearby as he had some free time before his scheduled speech.*

"Aren't you a stranger in this town, sir!" the shopkeeper asked.

"Sure, I'm a stranger," replied Twain.

"We're having a good lecture here tonight, sir," said the shopkeeper. "A 'Mark Twain' lecture. Are you going to attend it?"

"Why not? I will," said Twain.

"Do you have your ticket?" asked the shopkeeper.

"No, not yet," said Twain.

"That's bad. Because all seats are already sold; you'll have to stand," the shopkeeper said.

"Dear me," said Twain, "it seems as if I always have to stand when I like to hear that guy Twain lecture!"

Gandhiji's Railway Travel

☺ *Gandhiji often said that he had been able to live only because of his Sense of Humor; otherwise, he said, he would have committed suicide long ago.*

Once a journalist asked Gandhiji why he chose to travel by the third class compartments of the Indian railways, they being so dirty and crowded. Gandhiji smiled and said, "What can I do? There is no fourth class over there!"

Gandhiji's passion to live like a common Indian citizen was so great that he ate, slept, dressed, and traveled like a common countryman.

Abraham Lincoln (a)

☺ *Abraham Lincoln's great love for Humor is as famous as his other great qualities of helpfulness, simplicity, kindness to others, courage, etc. During his 1846 campaign for Congress, Lincoln attended a prayer service led by the Methodist minister, Rev. Peter Cartwright, who also happened to be his rival candidate. The speaker called on all who wished to go to Heaven to stand up. All except Lincoln stood up.*

"I'm grieved" said Cartwright, "to see Abe Lincoln sitting back there unmoved by appeals. If he doesn't want to go to Heaven and doesn't want to escape Hell, will he tell where he does want to go?"

Lincoln stood up slowly and said, "I'm going to Congress!" and walked out.

Abraham Lincoln (b)

☺ *During a reception at the White House when Abraham Lincoln was President, one guest, while taking leave, waved his hat at Lincoln and said loudly, "Mr President, I'm from up in York state, where we believe that God Almighty and Abraham Lincoln are going to save this country."*

Jovially the President waved back at him and said, "My friend, you're half right!"

General Grant

☺ *General Ulysses Grant was Abraham Lincoln's most competent General and was also his favorite, to the chagrin of a number of powerful and influential politicians. These people repeatedly complained to the President that Grant was a drunkard. One day Lincoln asked them, "So Grant gets drunk, does he?"*

"Yes, he does, and we can prove it," was their reply.

"Well," said Lincoln, "you needn't waste your time regarding any proof; just find out which brand of whiskey Grant drinks, because I want to send a barrel of that liquor to each of my generals!"

When you have identified your comedy style and have decided to develop it in your own unique way, the next important step is to prepare yourself for delivering Humor. This in turn consists of two areas of ground work.

(1) Audience
(2) Text Material

Audience

In order to decide what you want to say, it is obvious that you should know whom you are addressing, what their viewpoints are, what their underlying interests are, their education, age group, gender ratio, occupation, religious leaning, political loyalties, and other such information. Detailed knowledge of the audience helps you not only to fine-tune the Humor part of your talk, but also to refine your main presentation. You therefore know their reservations and apprehensions, and so would be able to comprehensively cover them in your talk. You can use the language of the audience in your Humor, their jargon, buzzwords, acronyms, slang, etc., so that the touch of familiarity invites them to enjoy the Humor with an open mind. You'll also find it easy to steer clear of any offensive Humor as you know your listeners well. In short, knowing more about your audience is a step which is neglected only by a reckless speaker.

Text Material

To be able to use only relevant Humor in your presentation means you should have at your disposal, a large collection of humorous material. Collecting Humor is a very good habit as it encourages you to read Humor on a regular basis. Newspapers, magazines, periodicals, books, talks, internet, and TV are some of the resources from which you can liberally draw and build your own Humor library. Your library will make your search for the most appropriate piece of Humor for your presentation a lot easier and more enjoyable. Any collection, if it is to be of ready use, has to be numbered, indexed, and arranged so as to facilitate ready retrieval. Use of computers for this purpose is a very prudent step and can pay rich dividends.

Anecdotes

One of the most popular pieces of Humor, which has been in use for ages, are the anecdotes. Anecdotes are short stories (real or imaginary or partly both), which effectively bring out an idea.

These anecdotes were called parables centuries ago and have been used by speakers of every age. Two such early ones are given here.

Demosthenes' Parable

☺ *This one is said to have been used by the Greek thinker and orator, Demosthenes, when the gathered Athenians were in no mood to listen to his philosophy. But the same crowd was eager to hear the story with rapt attention.*

"A youth hired a donkey on one summer's day to go from his village to his fields nearby. At noon the sun was very hot, so the youth thought of sitting in the shade of the donkey. But the owner of the donkey also wanted to sit in the same shade. The youth said that as he had hired the donkey the shade belonged to him, but the owner disputed this claim saying that he had hired out only the donkey and not his shade!"

Saying these words Demosthenes started walking away, but the crowd would not allow him to go. They were extremely curious to know the outcome. Demosthenes chided them about how they were eager to know the fate of the shadow of a donkey even though it did not matter to them, but were indifferent to their own fate although that was the most important thing in life to them.

The people blushed at their own foolishness and listened to Demosthenes without any more fuss.

True Friendship

☺ *Two friends were discussing their money matters. Suddenly one of them asked the other, "What would you ask for if God appeared before you to give you your wish?"*

"All that I would ask for would be a very large heap of gold," replied the other.

The first one continued his questioning: "If you really got your heap of gold, would you give me, your close friend, a sizable share?"

The other friend sternly asked, "Do you think that I am such a fool? Why should I give you any share?"

His friend said, "Oh! We have been such good friends."

"So what? Why can't you get your own heap of gold, just like me, instead of pestering me?"

Here are two more anecdotes of a more recent origin.

Bringer of Bad Luck!

☺ *Madhu was a gambler who had lost all his wealth and would borrow from friends and relatives. He would borrow Rs 100 from anyone who took pity on him and in no time would make a beeline for the gambling rooms in the basement. One day, when he was standing at the entrance of* a departmental store, the owner of the store happened to walk by. He gave Rs 100 to Madhu. The next day, the same man gave Madhu another Rs 100. Soon this became a daily routine. As luck would have it, Madhu was losing the money everyday and his hopes of earning a fortune remained unfulfilled. So Madhu sought the advice of a friend who said, "You know Madhu, it is that owner of the store who is bringing you bad luck. Just avoid him the whole of next week!"

Plays, but doesn't Know How to!

☺ A businessman was complaining about his son-in-law to his friend and business colleague. "Well, my bloody son-in-law Ramesh can't drink and he can't play cards."

The friend said, "Why, that's fine. That's the kind of son-in-law to have. Isn't it?"

"No, No," said the first, "He can't play cards but plays! And he can't drink, but he drinks!"

Personal Anecdotes

When you include a funny personal experience into your talk, it is a very powerful way of adding Humor. Your own anecdote scores because of two main factors. First, because it is your own story, you will have very little problem in presenting it forcefully. There will be no fear of you forgetting any part of the story. Second, the anecdote is about an actual experience in life and hence will appeal to the audience like nothing else. Your readiness to share your personal experience with the listeners enhances their regard towards you; they also get closer to you because of the familiarity the anecdote builds. The chasm between you and the audience is covered to a large extent and this is a very positive development in favor of your presentation. The material for personal anecdotes is abundantly available to everyone; recollecting them, polishing them, relating the selected ones to your presentation—these are the steps which have to be attended to with care. Some incidents which could become interesting anecdotes include the following: your most embarrassing moment, your first day at work, your first customer, your first driving lesson, the biggest blunder you ever made, your funniest business meeting, your job interviews, the funniest teacher you had, the most helpless moment you have experienced, your funny encounters with strangers, etc. All these could be potential gold mines of healthy Humor. So go and hunt for the treasure.

When you use anecdotes of famous personalities, you are the best judge of whether to keep the names in them as they are or to change them to give the local touch. A Mahatma Gandhi anecdote may make your talk more impressive when used in its original form, whereas when the story is about a lesser known person it could be altered to suit your surroundings. It is not surprising to come across the same story attributed to different personalities. For example, the following story about two Japanese men in recent years, was originally a classic about two Greek merchants a few decades ago.

Japanese Humor

☺ *Once, two Japanese traders happened to meet at the Osaka railway station. The first one asked the other as to where he was going. The second trader didn't like the question, probably because he felt that the other was being too nosey. With a grimace, he said that he was going to Tokyo. The first trader said, "By saying that you are going to Tokyo you want me to believe that you are going to Kobe, but I'm not going to be easily fooled. I've already made enquiries and know that you are really going to Tokyo."*

Customizing the Text

Never make use of any joke or funny story in your talk in the form in which you read it in a book or a magazine. Study that piece of Humor as well as your main presentation material; apply your mind to decide the best place and manner in which the Humor piece can be smoothened into your talk; it has to be blended carefully. The relationship the story has with the topic has to be briefly explained first. The original story may be altered so that it suits your presentation. If the words and phrases in the original joke are troublesome, replace them with the ones you feel comfortable with. Modify it into a conversational style, which makes it easy to deliver. Make sure that you are not going to get stuck on the pronunciation of any of the words in the joke. Even while telling a joke which you have mastered through repeated telling, try experimenting a bit to make it a new joke each time. If the original story is about Napoleon and his soldiers, you may use it regarding your boss and his deputies. If it is about shepherds, you can use it using the welders in your shop instead. An incident during your air travel can be related to your recent railway travel or vice versa; add some specific details regarding date, time, place etc., if they are vague in the original. Your story should try to project a graphic picture of what you are telling. A clear picture is remembered longer than a fuzzy, ambiguous one. Instead of saying "Three men met at the club," say, "Sachin Tendulkar, Amitabh Bachchan, and Johny Walker happened to meet." Instead of saying that you were traveling by train, say, "I was traveling by the Deccan Queen from Mumbai to Pune." You may even make alterations in the subject matter of the story to suit it to the occasion you have in mind. In fact, one story can provide you with more than 10 stories based on it. Instead of the donkey and its shadow, you may be talking about a horse and its rein, or a house and its garden, an office building and its compound, etc. Remember how the clever Portia made use of a similar ploy to turn the tables on Shylock, the merchant of Venice?

Never announce that you are going to tell a funny story. All humorous items have to glide smoothly into your presentation unannounced. This is one of the most important rules regarding Humor. This is as important as the other rule of having a specific purpose for every piece of Humor you include. When such a purposeful piece of Humor is presented without prior notice, the surprise element makes it all the more enjoyable.

Do not be discouraged if your joke does not get the expected response. Try to understand what needs improvement. Try out different words, gestures, intonations, additional details, removal of unnecessary words and the like. Try to transform the failure into success. If you do not succeed with all these repeated improvements, opt for a new story and begin at the beginning. Keep on trying till you succeed. Then you can try the same with another story and still another. Gradually, you will see your collection growing into a large repertoire. You can now add Humor to any of your speechs with confidence.

You may, at this point, wonder as to the proper amount of Humor in any speech and where it should be added. There are no hard and fast rules governing these factors. You should not lose sight of the fact that Humor is not what takes you to the podium; it is only an accessory which helps make your main message powerful, convincing, and memorable. Humor is also there to relieve monotony and add some fun. You can decide, depending upon your topic, the duration, frequency, positioning and quantum of Humor. Be alert to the reactions of the audience and decide your course of action.

Delivery

Reciting a joke for maximum benefit calls attention to a few important steps. The most important thing is that you should be full of enthusiasm when you are about to tell a joke. As already stated, to be successful, every piece of Humor depends on that little surprise element. The initial building up of the story aims at guiding the listeners in one routine direction and prepares them to expect what is going to be said next. The speaker speaks in a very normal manner when he covers this portion of the story. It is like herding all the listeners on to the center of the rug. When every listener is positioned on the rug, the punch line of the joke is stated by the speaker; generally this is the line which surprises and even shocks the listeners. It is analogous to pulling the rug off from under the feet of the unsuspecting listeners instantaneously. Naturally, there is a split-second delay in the listeners understanding the exact meaning of the punch line, which is actually the climax of the story. Soon the listeners will break into laughter. The speaker, therefore, after uttering the punch line, should pause briefly to allow the audience to understand, appreciate, and enjoy the joke. Whatever else happens, the speaker should not be tempted to explain the joke to anyone in the audience. The talk may be resumed after the laughter subsides.

Given ahead are two jokes with their punch lines marked in bold.

Last Wish!

☺ *The doctor looked at the patient and became very grave. He said to the patient, "Mr Ganesh, I'll be very frank with you. You are almost at the final stage and I'm sorry that medicine can do very little to improve your condition.... Now that you have heard me, do you wish to see anyone in particular?"*

   *"Yes," said the patient in a very feeble voice, and beckoned the doctor to come nearer. When the doctor bent and placed his ear very close to the mouth of the patient, all that the latter said was, "**Another doctor!**"*

UN Survey

☺ *A few years ago, the UN was organizing a worldwide opinion poll. They put one question to all the member countries: "Would you please give your honest opinion on what would be the solution to the food shortage in the rest of the world?"*

   The poll turned out to be a disaster because, in Africa, they didn't know what food was; in Eastern Europe they didn't know what "honest" was; in Western Europe they didn't know what "shortage" was; in China they didn't *know what "opinion" was; in the Middle East they didn't know what "solution" was; and **in the US they didn't know what "rest of the world" was!***

Conclusion

Jokes are certainly very popular, but an unrelated and untimely joke is a big embarrassment to everyone. Humor has a variety of forms and types and hence, for maximum effectiveness, you have to recognize which variety suits you best. Just as you need time, effort, and patience for preparing your main speech, the Humor you choose to use in your speech also requires careful selection, modification, adaptation, customizing, and rehearsed delivery on the basis of detailed analysis of your topic, audience, organizers, and latest developments pertaining to these factors. Do not be discouraged if you meet with failure in the beginning; keep experimenting and persevering until you achieve repeated success.

Chapter 7

Humor in Extraordinary Situations

"If you don't learn to laugh at trouble, You won't have anything to laugh at, when you grow old!"

—Ed Howe

Hostility

You can never be sure that hostility will not raise its ugly head in your workplace. There can be very little immunity from a hostile question. A good speaker always anticipates that no matter how well-received his presentation may be, any person in the audience can destroy all that peace and tranquility by raising a single hostile question. In this situation, the audience who, until now, appeared to be agreeing to all the points you made, shows no hesitation in backing up the solo questioner and pressing you for a convincing reply to that all-important question. Let's look at the following example.

Tackling Hostility

Suppose you are making a presentation about a new gadget developed by you, its market potential, and the profit the product line is likely to bring to the company in the coming years. Your presentation was welcomed with loud applause after which someone raises a question: "What happened to the Model SQT-40 which you talked about last year?"

Immediately you will see in everyone's eyes, the eagerness for an answer. You know that the Model SQT-40 did not fare well in the marketplace and had to be discontinued. If you tamely disclose this information, your presentation about the new product line would almost be a waste of your effort because your listeners will most likely conclude that the new product line will also suffer a fate similar to the Model SQT-40. If you dismiss the question with a loud artificial laugh, perhaps you will seem to be concealing some important facts from the group. If you give wrong or false information, you run the risk of being nailed down sooner or later. Humor can save you from this predicament.

Suppose you say in a lighter vein, "As the Model SQT-40 gadgets were found to attract tsunamis and earthquakes, we had to keep their production on hold till new versions which are immune to these disasters are developed.

But to give a serious reply to your very important question, the US market for our SQT-40 has been flooded by Chinese models at an artificial price which cannot cover our material costs. This can only be a short-term tactic by the Chinese. We are working on ways and means of taking on the Chinese at their own game, by adding special features to our standard model. The proto-types of these are under life-span testing."

With this answer you can get back to your original agenda.

The most important point in situations like the one just discussed is to anticipate the hostile questions and to be ready with both witty and serious answers. Humor removes the edge from the hostile question, eases pent up passions, and prepares listeners to accept the serious answers with composure. Merely laughing away a serious question with a comic reply is totally improper. The questioner feels being put to shame. Also, such a response may provoke other people in the group to sympathize with the questioner and rally behind him; your credibility will take a big hit.

Political leaders all over the world are masters of these kinds of situations. Let's look at a few examples.

Ronald Reagan

☺ *Ronald Reagan at a news conference in Washington DC on 28 September 1982:*

Reporter: "Mr President, in talking about the continuing recession tonight, you have blamed the mistakes of the past and you've blamed the Congress. Does any of the blame belong to you?"

Ronald Reagan: "Yes, because for many years I was a Democrat!"

As Sound as a Dollar!

☺ *Press reporter: "Isn't the dollar very weak?"*

Joseph Wahed: "That reminds me of what my doctor said to me when I went for a check-up. He said to me 'You're as sound as the dollar!'"

(Joseph Wahed was the Chief Economist of Wells Fargo Bank.)

Michael Eisner

☺ *Michael Eisner, Chairman, Walt Disney Company, was once asked a question which was not hostile, but tricky.*

"Mr Eisner, which is your favorite ride: Disneyland or Disney World?"

"The stock market!" replied Eisner.

(Eisner, being the CEO, could not afford to be seen to prefer one ride to the other.)

Humor, if properly used, does not only deflect hostility, it also leaves pleasant memories. Psychological research gives us a very important guideline in our interpersonal relationships. Suppose two persons have a dialogue in the office. After a few weeks both of them are likely to forget the exact words spoken and their chronological order; but they are most likely to remember how they felt during the dialogue—tense, relieved, threatened, amused, etc.—and whether the dialogue was friendly, enjoyable, worthy of having it again, or something to be totally forgotten. Humor makes these memories pleasant and helps to reinforce personal relationships even when they faced some rough weather in the initial stages. Following is an example.

Anticipating Aggression

☺ *A telephone company executive was addressing a customers' gathering organized by the company for improving public relations. She made a very impressive presentation about the new facilities being provided by the company, the widening of their network, and the improvement in the reliability of service provided. After the presentation, the invitees were free to raise questions. One question asked by a particularly loud customer was: "The company is making more and more profits every year, but the long-distance call rates are shooting upward. Is this not totally unfair?"*

The telephone company had anticipated such questions and had trained their executives to handle them. The executive said, "I've got good news as well as bad news. The bad news is that you are correct when you said that the long-distance call rates are going up. The good news is that all the countries in the world are drifting closer and so distances are getting reduced!"

> *When this humorous reply was received well by the
> audience, the executive went on to explain how the improved
> and more reliable services would have cost even more and
> how the company's efficiency drive has contained the rise in
> costs within very reasonable limits.*

Anticipation and preparation are the most important steps
to combat hostility. Hostility is a human trait which cannot
be wished away in work situations. People turn hostile
toward you even when you are not at fault. People lose
their temper for a variety of reasons and all of them are not
always rational however much you may like them to be.
Don't you get angry with someone even though he has not
contributed in anyway to your ill temper? For example,

Tax Forms and Toys!

> ☺ *Someone asked the central finance minister as to why the
> tax forms were so complex. He smiled and said, "Because
> they were drafted by the same people who draft instructions
> for assembling children's toys!"*

Robert S. McNamara

> ☺ *During the 1950s, the Ford Motor Company suffered
> big losses in the marketplace. Closure of plant after plant
> was adopted to cut down the losses. This led to large-scale
> employee separations and hostility between management and
> employee unions. It was strongly rumored that the accounts
> people had the final say in this matter, even though all other
> departmental heads were against plant closures.*

The company president, Robert S. McNamara, called a meeting of the top executives to discuss a proposal from the accounts people to close down yet another plant. One very senior technical executive objected strongly and asked; "If closure of this plant is going to improve our situation, we can extend this logic and close down all the existing plants as well. Then, instead of minimizing losses, would we not have zero loss?"

This hostile question could not be answered properly by the proponents of plant closure. It was finally decided not to close any more plants. The company started taking other turn-around activities and very soon was on the way to making profits.

Reducing Budget Size

☺ *An executive submitted his departmental budget for the forthcoming year to his boss for approval. The boss wanted a cutting down of the budgetary provisions so the executive trimmed down the provisions and re-submitted the budget. The boss once again asked for a further reduction. This went on another three to four times. Finally, the exasperated executive got the budget papers reduced to the size of a postal stamp and submitted them with a note saying this was the only type of reduction now possible. The boss laughed loudly and approved the budget without any further queries.*

How often do you have a confrontation with your peers at the workplace? When the arguments become vehement, you may think of applying a Humor-brake. Crack a joke and allow laughter to cool tempers. You can pick up a neutral but relevant subject for the joke like the marketplace, a fussy customer, the latest development in the city, etc. This will help in preventing any further escalation of the conflict. After this, you may try to talk about the areas of agreement. Take a look at the following examples.

Uprightness can be Dangerous

☺ *Congressman John Allen was campaigning for votes in a somewhat hostile area; a heavy stone was thrown at him. Fortunately, Allen bent down to receive a flower from a small girl and the stone missed him. "You see," he said to those who started congratulating him on his lucky escape, "had I been an upright politician, I would have been killed today!"*

Communist Reply

☺ *There was a meeting in one of the provinces of the erstwhile Soviet bloc. One of the party members, Comrade Popsky got up and asked, "Comrade leader, I have only three questions. If we are the greatest industrial nation in the world, what happened to our automobiles?*

If we have the best agriculture in the world, what happened to our bread?

If we are the finest cattle breeders in the world, what happened to our meat?"

The presiding chairman stared at Comrade Popsky, hardly believing what he had heard. Then he answered, "It is too late to answer your questions tonight. I will answer them fully in our next meeting."

When the party members met the following week, there was only one question raised by the audience: "What happened to Comrade Popsky?"

Fortunately, this type of answering of hostile questions need not be emulated by you!

Humor in Negotiations

Business people are frequently required to display their skills at the negotiation table from time to time. Very few persons are confident of their own negotiating skills to be comfortable. Any negotiation involves certain demands at the negotiating table which are contradictory. There is no known formula which can be applied as a basis of agreement. For becoming a good negotiator you have to be tough but sensitive, analytical but flexible, know where to push and also when to retreat. Yet, there is no ideal mix of these which can suit every situation. Each negotiation is different. Every organization values their star negotiators. There is a constant need for negotiating. Inter-company deals involving mergers and acquisitions, labor union-management negotiations, legal battles with outside entities, and many such situations crop up almost on a regular basis. When opposing groups are in dialogue, Humor can play a vital role in establishing a good atmosphere conducive to "give and take." It can act as a pressure-relief valve when tensions rise beyond safe limits. Humor also helps the participants to humanize and to see a larger perspective of win-win relationships. See the example below.

Ariel Sharon

☺ *The Prime Minister of Israel, Ariel Sharon, sits down with the Palestinian leader Yasser Arafat at the beginning of the* negotiations regarding the resolution of the conflict between the two nations. Sharon requests that he be allowed to begin with a story. Arafat gives his consent readily.

"Years before the Israelites came to the Promised Land and settled here, Moses led them for 40 years through the desert. The Israelites began complaining that they were thirsty and lo and behold, a miracle occurred and a stream of water appeared before them. They drank the water and then decided to bathe. Moses also bathed and when he came out of the water his clothing was missing."

"It was the Palestinians," said the Israelites.

"Wait a minute," objected Arafat immediately. "There were no Palestinians during the time of Moses."

"All right," replied Sharon. "Now that we've got that settled, let's begin our negotiations."

It would be prudent to remember as a negotiator that a win–win agreement is the most desirable result, as it would ensure healthy long-term relationships between the negotiating parties. Listening to what the opposing party members say holds the key to a better understanding of their viewpoints. Additionally, your focused listening entitles you to the privilege of being well listened to, when you speak. Look at the following example.

Give and Take

☺ The management and the workers' union of a Pune-based engineering company were negotiating the demands put forward by the workers' union. The list of demands placed by the workers' union was termed "exhorbitant" by the management, who highlighted the fact that the monthly wages and other benefits paid by the company were already the highest in Pune. *The workers' union admitted that this was true, but because a number of neighboring companies had declared a rise in the wage package, they too felt they should be given the same. The union secretary drew the attention of the management to the fact that negotiations involved "give and take." The personnel manager caught hold of this phrase and said, "Sadubhau, you are suggesting tossing the coin to decide the issue by insisting on a 'heads, we win and tails, you lose' rule. Your 'give and take' insists that 'we give and you take.' Don't you think that you should now talk about what you are going to give?"*

The union leaders laughed at these words and the discussions thereon focused on the raising of productivity and to productivity-linked incentives. A final settlement was reached during the same week.

—Mohan Kulkarni

Staging a Walkout

☺ *Recently outside the negotiation room of a company, a labor union representative suggested the following to the personnel manager, "I've an idea. Before we start negotiating, let's both practice walking out in disgust!"*

Making a Pact

☺ *The election date was fast approaching. The contest was essentially between two election-scarred veterans. One evening they happened to meet at a party thrown by a common friend, who suggested to them to resort to clean and cultured campaigning, free from mudslinging. Both opponents, in*

> *deference to the advice given, shook hands and made a pact.*
> *The first one said, "Let us be friends. Even though we contest,*
> *I promise that I will stop telling lies about you."*
>
> *The other one smiled and said, "I am game for it. From*
> *now onward I will stop telling the truth about you!"*

"Negotiation is no laughing matter," states Ed Brodow, who happens to be a strong believer in the use of Humor in negotiations. According to Brodow, Humor confers three important advantages. Humor brightens up things; it enables you to be tough without offending the other party; and it is of great help in dodging awkward questions. For example,

Driving Tension Out

> ☺ *According to a report published in* Time *magazine, an*
> *American pilot who happened to enter North Korean airspace,*
> *was shot down and captured. The US government was very*
> *keen to secure the man's release and hence started negotiating*
> *with their North Korean counterparts. When the chief*
> *American negotiator met with the North Korean authorities,*
> *he asked, "Well, is he okay? Does he still have his fingernails?"*
>
> *This was a totally unexpected question. It took the North*
> *Koreans by surprise for a moment, after which they all*
> *laughed loudly. The tension in the room had been driven out*
> *by that one remark.*

Saying "NO" with Humor

When anyone approaches you requesting a favor, refusing them is always very difficult and unpleasant. You can explain very logically how the request does not comply with company policy or current regulations; or how this precedent could lead to the opening of a Pandora's box; but the other person usually becomes unduly upset as he interprets this refusal as a personal rejection and hence a personal insult. You may not be very happy to see the person you consider your right hand get offended. In order to prevent such a predicament, a touch of Humor along with your refusal would be very effective. By employing this method, you confirm that you value the person very much, even though regrettably his request may not be approved. For example,

Cut Me into Pieces

☺ *The vice president, marketing, had informed his assistants of his refusal to a common request which had been put to him by them. He called them for a meeting and had got placed before each seat a copy of his photograph and a pair of scissors. He said to them, "I know how you may be feeling about me. Go ahead and cut me into tiny pieces in one go."*

With these words the boss conveyed the message that he was sensitive to the feelings of his people; his gesture also made his people understand how hard it had been for him to disapprove of their requests. In short, they would understand his "NO" clearly and could rationally discuss how the pending problems could be solved.

Lincoln, the Lion Tamer

☺ *After being elected President, Abraham Lincoln's regime was inaugurated in March, 1861. Despite this achievement, some government properties in the South like Fort Sumter,*

Fort Pickens, etc., were still vulnerable. Some of Lincoln's advisers recommended that Lincoln yield these properties to the enemy. Lincoln said to them, "There's a lesson for all of us in the fable of the lion and the woodcutter's daughter. 'A lion fell in love with a woodcutter's daughter. He went to the girl's father and demanded that the girl be given to him in marriage. The woodcutter readily agreed but said that the lion's claws were too fearsome and should be first removed. So the lion got his claws taken out. Next, it was the turn of the fierce teeth to be extracted. Now when the toothless and clawless lion came to stake his claim for the girl, the woodcutter beat him black and blue.'"

"I do not want to give up my properties like the foolish lion," said Lincoln.

Giving Chance to Others

☺ *A prominent Washington woman sought an appointment with the President to demand that her son be appointed as a colonel. She said, "Mr President, my son's grandfather fought the British at Lexington. The boy's father took part in the Battle of Monterey in Mexico. This proves that the service record of our family qualifies him for that post."*

"I agree, madam," replied Lincoln. "Your family has done enough for the country. It's time to give someone else a chance!"

Doorkeeper's Qualifications

☺ *A member of the Republican Party with no other qualification once approached Abraham Lincoln and said, "Mr President, please appoint me as the doorkeeper of the House."*

Lincoln asked him, "Have you any experience in doorkeeping?"

"No," said the candidate.

"Well, are you quite familiar with the theory of doorkeeping?"

"To be frank, no."

"Have you attended any lectures on doorkeeping?"

"No, nobody told me to."

"Perhaps you might have read some good books on doorkeeping?"

"Unfortunately, I haven't."

"Do you still think that you have the proper qualifications to become a doorkeeper?"

"No sir, I can see that I am not fit for the post." Saying this the candidate made a hasty exit.

Neighborly Pact

☺ There was a small shop in one corner adjoining the compound of a scheduled bank. The shop sold newspapers, magazines, tobacco products, etc. One day, a friend of the shopkeeper barged into the shop and demanded a loan of Rs 1,000 for just one week. The shopkeeper didn't want to lose any money as he knew his friend's habits well, but he also didn't want to lose the friendship. So he said, "Subash, I'd have readily lent you the money and the amount you are asking for is not very big either, but I have entered into a 'No-Competition-Contract' with the bank here; according to the contract, the bank cannot sell newspapers or tobacco products and I can't lend any money to people!"

Humor to Handle
Unwarranted Insults

Very often you come across situations in which you are insulted without any justification. If the insult is hurled at you by your enemy or by someone whom you do not rate as significant it is best that you ignore it totally. But when the adverse remarks are made by someone who is important, someone whom you respect, or someone whom you don't know well enough to be discourteous, you are advised not to ignore such remarks. If you ignore them that person may continue to harbor a misjudged poor opinion about you. If you try to correct him in a civil manner, his ego may not allow him to accept your correction. In such situations if you display your strong reaction cloaked in equally strong Humor, the final outcome may be useful for both of you. Following are a few examples of such a situation.

Ernst Rutherford

☺ *A journalist once went to Lord Ernst Rutherford, the famous physicist who discovered the atomic nucleus and asked him for help in preparing a write-up on the nuclear structure of matter aimed at the education of ordinary people. Rutherford laughed at the journalist's idea and said that the subject was too complex to be explained to ordinary people. But the visitor was not to be put off so quickly. He maintained that if a genius like Lord Rutherford cooperated with a committed writer like himself, the task could be achieved. Rutherford got very angry with this assertion and threw a copy of a scientific paper, which included complex scientific calculations at the journalist with this challenge, "If you are so confident about your ability, you translate this paper into your ordinary language and publish it in your three-penny paper."*

The journalist glanced at the article and saw he couldn't understand anything. He coolly tore off a sheet from his short-hand notebook and tossing it on the table said, "Let's agree to this, sir. You translate my writing and I'll do yours."

Rutherford, though short-tempered, was also a humorist at heart. He liked the resourcefulness of the journalist and guided him in his writing.

Thomas Huxley

☺ *Charles Darwin, enunciator of the theory of evolution, had to face stiff opposition from the Vatican for this theory. Thomas Huxley happened to be the strongest upholder of Darwin's theory, and naturally, he also earned the hostility of the church. Once, in a gathering of leading scientists of the world held in England, Huxley made a very forceful and highly convincing presentation of the theory. He was taken to task by Archbishop Samuel Wilburforce who taunted Huxley saying, "Professor, you have very effectively proved that you are a descendant of the apes, but I have a doubt. Is this descedency from your father's side or mother's side?"*

Huxley immediately retorted, "I consider myself extremely lucky that I have descended from apes rather than from Bishops who while behaving senselessly consider themselves very intelligent. It is the same the from father's side as well as mother's side."

Paid in the Same Coin

☺ *A very poor Chinese man operated a small laundry next door to a prosperous restaurant. Everyday, he would take his* home-cooked bowl of rice, place his chair as near as he dared to the restaurant and while he ate, he would enjoy sniffing the appetizing aromas from the restaurant.

One day, the rich restaurant owner took the laundryman to task and handed him a bill "for the smell of food." The poor man first thought that it was a joke; but when the restaurant owner called his men to seize the poor fellow, he said, "Wait a minute; I'll get the money."

He went to his laundry, caught hold of the cash box and brought it to the restaurant owner. The laundryman shook the cash box and the coins therein made a lot of noise. The laundryman now said, "Well, I have paid with the sound of my money for the smell of your food! Is it okay?"

The people in the restaurant who had crowded at the entrance, laughed loudly and said that the greed of the restaurant owner has been properly repaid by the wit of the laundryman.

Honest Answer!

☺ A newly recruited constable had to face an enquiry before the inspector. The charge was that he had used derogatory language with his boss, the sub-inspector.

"Sir" the accused cried out, "what is wrong in my answering a question?"

"Which question? What do you mean?" snarled the inspector.

"He asked me, 'Do you know who I am?' and I told him 'you're a damned bloody fool!'"

Winston Churchill

☺ George Bernard Shaw once sent a letter to Winston Churchill.

"I'm enclosing two tickets for the opening night of my play. Please attend and bring a friend if you have one."

Churchill responded with a telegram: "I can't attend your play on the opening night. I plan to come to the second night, if you have one."

Mao Tse-Tung

☺ *Nikita Khrushchev is out walking a goat, when Mao-Tse-Tung comes along and asks, "Why are you walking with that pig?"*

Khrushchev answers, "You idiot! This isn't a pig, it's a goat."

Mao replies, "I wasn't talking to you!"

Mind and Matter

☺ *A top-ranking British official once entertained a haughty and sophisticated lady in his home. Inadvertently, his assistant asked her to sit on the left side of her host rather than at his right hand, the place of honor. The visitor was offended and became very indignant. Turning to her host she complained bitterly about the seating arrangement. The host replied, "It is a very small matter. I have found by long experience that those who mind don't matter and those who matter don't mind!"*

Humor with Your Boss

It is always in your own interest to keep your boss well humored. Your career progress, whether you like it or not, depends to a significant degree on the relationship between you and your boss. Accept this fact of life and maximize your efforts to make this relationship very rich and fruitful. It would be to your advantage if you carefully study the traits and qualities of your boss in some detail. As your aim is to make the two-person team of you and your boss superstrong, successful, and spectacular, your clear understanding of the likes and dislikes, the strengths and weaknesses of your boss will enable you to work in such a way that you please him much more frequently than give cause for irritation. You would be prudent to work for maximum advantage with the strengths of your boss and also to compensate, with your efforts, the weaknesses that your boss may have, making them insignificant. Remember that it would benefit you to make your boss happy and effective; never entertain thoughts of competing with him or of "teaching him a lesson." Your boss will treat you like his "treasure," when he is convinced that you do not pose any threat to him and that you are there to enhance his strengths and to neutralize his weaknesses. Keep the lines of regular communication clear and open so that misunderstandings are promptly cleared and the boss's guidance regularly received; two-way information flow is timely and candid. It is also important to remember that in the unlikely case you think your boss is an incorrigible sadist, fire your boss and seek a new job! Let's look at some examples.

Frederick the Great

☺ *Frederick the Great sent a messenger with a letter to one of his generals. The letter read: "I send you against the enemy with 60,000 men."*

When the troops were counted they numbered only 50,000. When the general referred this matter to Frederick, he got this reply: "There is no mistake. I counted you as 10,000 men. I am sure you will rise up to my expectations."

Alex Haley

☺ *Alex Haley, the author of the TV series "Roots", had a picture in his office with a turtle sitting atop a fence. The picture was there to remind him that he was where he was because he was just like the turtle who got up on that fence because of the help of others. (Remember with gratitude your bosses.)*

Benjamin Disraeli

☺ *Queen Victoria said of William Gladstone, "When I'm with him, I feel I am with one of the most important leaders in the world."*

But of Benjamin Disraeli she said, "He makes me feel that I am one of the most important leaders of the world."

Anniversary of Salary Rise!

☺ *An office worker slicing a gaily decorated cake at his desk, said to his boss, "Hope you don't mind, sir. Just a little celebration on the tenth anniversary of my last salary rise!"*

Humor can be of great help to you in teaming up with your boss. If you have a good Sense of Humor, it proves that you are happy and that you like your job. To make

FIGURE 9
Humor and the Boss

your boss laugh, you have to be fully relaxed and extremely enthusiastic. Study and try and find out what amuses your boss. Does he like jokes, cartoons, puns, anecdotes, quips? This knowledge will enable you to use his type of Humor when you interact with him. But be warned: even if your boss indulges in telling off-colour jokes, do not make the mistake of emulating him in this respect. Following are some examples.

Serving Both Ways

☺ *Boss: "Do you know how to serve customers?"*
New recruit: "Yes of course, I can serve them either way."
Boss: "What do you mean … either way?"
New recruit: "So that they'll come back or they won't!"

Sankaran Nair

☺ *The late Sankaran Nair resigned in disgust from the viceroy's executive council. Lord Chelmsford, the then Viceroy, asked him if he could suggest someone who could take his place. "Yes," replied Nair. Pointing to his peon, Ramprasad, Nair said, "He is tall, he is handsome, he wears his livery well and he will say 'yes' to whatever you say. Altogether he will make an ideal member of the Viceroy's council!"*

One More Idiot!

☺ *I was asked by my boss to explain why my quarterly report was behind schedule and included so many errors. I became indignant and said, "Sir, you have to understand that*

I have four idiots working under me! It's so difficult to get anything done by them in time, and correctly!"

He looked up from his desk and said, "You are lucky. I have five idiots working for me!"

☺ *The MD of a company gave a young manager a proposed training program for assessment. The manager completed the assignment and wrote a detailed two-and-a-half page, single-spaced memo outlining his thoughts. After wading through the paper, the MD scrawled, "So what?" across the face of the memo and shunted it right back to him.*

The next day the MD received a four-sentence summation and action recommendation from the manager, which told the MD everything he wanted to know.

MD and the Goldfish

☺ *The MD of a company kept a goldfish bowl on his desk. No, he was not particularly interested in fish, he explained to a visitor. "Its nice to have someone around here who opens his mouth without asking for a raise or an additional discount!" said the MD.*

Humor for Salespersons

In recent decades phenomenal progress has been achieved in the areas of:

(1) Quality improvement.
(2) Cost reduction.

(3) Higher quality service and support based on superior technology.

(4) Leaner organizations enabled by the spread of computer networks, global manufacturing, and outsourced service improvements.

Today, however, these factors are merely the prerequisites for entry into the marketplace; none of these or not even all of these together give you a competitive advantage. Today, the single most essential resource for gaining a competitive advantage is the quality of the sales personnel selling the product or service. For example,

Humouring the Customer

☺ *Job rotation was the "fashion of the day" in corporate circles to overcome business problems. In one company, they asked their head of the sales division, Subodh Datta, to take charge of the engineering division with immediate effect. In turn, they transferred the chief engineer, Sharad Joshi, to head the sales division. As a cautionary step, it was decided that both of them would jointly call on important customers, whenever large value contracts were to be negotiated. It was noticed that whenever Datta accompanied Joshi, the company would secure the contracts. But whenever, Datta failed to go with Joshi, those contracts would be won by the competitors. The MD called a review meeting in which this issue was discussed in detail. The conclusions were startling.*

(1) Datta and Joshi had very different approaches to the customer. For example, when a customer told them about a fierce wrestling contest that he saw, Joshi was sure to say that he had seen an even bigger and bloodier duel.

In a similar situation, Datta would say, how he wished that he had been there to see the contest.

(2) Whenever a customer narrated a joke, Datta would respond with spontaneous hearty laughter and would admire the joke saying it was a classic joke. Datta would not mind doing so, even though the same customer might have told him the same joke on three previous occasions. But Joshi being a straightforward, no-nonsense type of a man, would not find any fun in the joke, which he had already heard so many times.

Al the end of the meeting, Joshi made it a point to emulate Datta in future when he met customers and this step gave better order inflows to the company.

Amazing Salesmanship

☺ The owner of a Florida-based megastore called a newly recruited salesman one late evening and asked about the number of customers he had served that day. The salesman replied, "One, sir." The owner was dismayed to hear this and proceeded to ask about the value of the goods sold. He was amazed to hear a figure of $125,859 mentioned. Naturally, this called for a detailed explanation. The salesman was offered a cup of coffee and asked to sit down and explain how he had performed this miracle. The salesman said, "I happened to explain to that guy about the joy of fishing. He was impressed and bought a set of fishing tackle. I suggested that the coastline would be ideal for a powerfully-built person like him and described how a 6 m boat would suit his purpose. As his car was too small to tow the boat, I recommended the purchase of a larger vehicle in our auto division."

The astounded owner congratulated the salesman and exclaimed, "You sold all those things to a guy who came in just to buy a fishing hook, right?"

The owner was in for greater bewilderment and disbelief when the salesman said, "Actually he came here to buy some quick relief for his wife's migraine. I offered him my sympathy, now that his weekend would mean pigeon-holing with his none-too-well wife. When he asked for alternatives, I suggested he go fishing."

Resourceful Sales

☺ A plump lady entered a bookshop and asked the salesgirl whether she had the book, How to Lose Body Weight.

The girl said that all copies of that particular book had been sold out but that she had the book, How to Gain Body Weight, by the same author.

The lady was offended and angrily remarked, "Why are you making fun of me?"

The salesgirl apologized for the unintended offence and proceeded to explain. "Madam, I meant no offence. Just do the opposite of what this book prescribes."

The lady smiled and bought the book.

As the competition heats up, products and services move toward parity with one another. This development makes the quality of the sales force ever more important for the survival and success of the organization. The skills required and the approaches to be used by the salespersons depend on the customers; essentially two customer-related factors seem to matter most.

(1) How long (in terms of time) and how complex the purchase process is.

(2) What is the expertise of the purchaser in making the purchase involved? What is the experience?

Customer Taking Inventory

☺ *A woman visited every department of the new mega mall in Bangalore without spending a single rupee. One of the salesmen ventured to make a mild protest.*

"Madam," he asked, "are you shopping here?"

The woman looked surprised and replied, "Certainly: What else would I be doing?"

The salesman hesitated a bit and then babbled, "I thought that you were taking the inventory!"

Ingenious Sales

☺ *Peter Greene, who lived in Reading, England, got his first novel published. In the first six months, only 20 copies were sold. He then had an advertisement published in the dailies of the city which said: "Millionaire young writer seeks matrimony from eligible girls like the heroine in the recent novel, x x x x, written by Peter Greene."*

Before the week ended, all the copies of the book were sold out!

Speaking to Grover Whalen

☺ *Grover Whalen, during his administration of the New York World Fair, was known for his inaccessibility. One salesman, after repeated rebuffs, stormed past the secretary. The shocked girl called out, "You can't speak to Mr Whalen."*

The visitor just paused and said, "Young lady, do you know that I talk everyday, twice with God, The Almighty; he listens to me. I can therefore certainly speak to Mr Grover Whalen!"

He got the interview.

Clark Gable's Films

☺ *In the heydays of Hollywood, a salesman arrived in a small town in Venezula, South America, and tried to offer the latest Clark Gable pictures to a local cinema owner. The latter was in for a shock. He said, "But Clark Gable is dead."*

The salesman denied this.

"Yes, he is dead," insisted the Venezulan. "Didn't you see his last film in which he died? If you saw it, you must know."

The salesman said, "But it's only a film; he was acting!"

"Don't you believe what you've seen with your own eyes?" asked the cinema owner. "We saw him die. There would be a riot if we showed another Clark Gable picture!"

The Power of the Pen

☺ *The Parker pen company had a funny experience with one of their ads. They introduced a new pen with a unique ink; the ink did not leak under any circumstances. So, the company claimed this product would prevent embarrassing situations arising from ink stains. When they launched this new product worldwide, in some countries the word "embarrassment" was erroneously translated into 'embrazar,' which in the language there, meant averting pregnancy.*

The company was flooded with demands for the new wonder contraceptive and had to make hasty changes to their claims of the pen's powers.

According to surveys made, it is found that customers rank the desired qualities of salespeople as given ahead.

(1) A friendly disposition.
(2) Readiness to devote time to customers.
(3) Excellent ability to interface.
(4) A quality product/service.
(5) Thorough knowledge about point (4).
(6) Perseverance in work.

It is said that: "He who works with his hands is a laborer. He who works with his hands and his head is a craftsman; he who works with his hands, head, and heart is an artist; he who works with his hands, head, heart, and legs is a salesman!" (Droke, 1956).

Boosting Customer's ego

☺ *A company manufacturing male contraceptives were confounded when they were left with huge unsold stocks of the small and medium sizes of their product; added to this the demand for the large size ones exceeded their wildest dreams. The company had conducted an elaborate survey to establish their demand forecast and had spent considerable amounts of resources on the market survey. The marketing team held a number of brainstorming sessions to unravel the mystery.*

Following all these deliberations, the company decided to re-embark the campaign with the same three sizes; but now they were designated as Big, Super, and Jumbo! To their surprise and jubilation, the market response was in line with their demand forecast.

Know Your Customers

☺ *A market promotion project for a novel detergent powder fell flat in Saudi Arabia and baffled all the concerned executives. None could explain the reasons for this failure. The ad was plain and simple. A picture showed a heap of filthy clothing on the left, a lady with a triumphant smile in the middle, and a pile of neatly stacked, bright and spotless dresses on the right. After a good deal of investigations, discussions, and meetings one sharp guy recalled that the Saudis read from right to left!*

Tact in Selling

☺ *An elderly woman entered a shop and asked to be shown tablecloths. The salesman brought a huge heap and showed the lady good many tablecloths. The woman said that she had seen them elsewhere. She then asked, "Don't you have something new?"*

The resourceful salesman went to the basement and brought out another lot of tablecloths. While showing them he said, "These are the latest in design. See, how the border runs beautifully right round the edges; also, the centre is in the middle. Aren't these lovely?"

The woman was impressed and said, "Yes, yes! These are the ones I was looking for. I will buy six of these!"

If you want to succeed as a salesperson, you should like people. Humor can confer on you many advantages in your work. The benefits of Humor discussed in the earlier chapters need not be listed here again. For salespersons, Humor is of special interest because it breaks through the customers' established pattern of rejection. It enables them to retain their own perspective in spite of unfriendly, irritating, and hostile responses from customers. Humor helps in a big way by keeping the dialogues on track. Let's look at some examples.

Everything is Useful

☺ *A man looking for neck ties, carefully selected a dozen and rejected another dozen. The salesman carefully put the rejected ones into a separate box and marked it with an "L." The buyer was curious to know about the fate of those ties. The salesman smiled and said, "We'll sell them to the women who come in here to buy ties for men."*

Plenty to Suit You

☺ *A buxom lady entered a shop which was holding its annual sale. No garment seemed to suit her proportions. The lady seemed upset and the salesgirl was getting tired. The lady finally asked, "Don't you have anything which will suit me?"*

"Yes, madam," said the girl. "The umbrellas and handkerchiefs are downstairs; we've received new supplies only yesterday!"

What's a Pekingese!

☺ The salesman saw a pensive customer and so he asked, "What are you worrying about?"

The customer moaned, "My wife wants a Pekingese as her birthday gift, but I'm not able to find one for anything less than Rs 5,000. That is way above my budget."

"Don't worry," said the enthusiastic salesman. "I'm here to help you. You're right in saying that Rs 5,000 is too high a price. I'll get it to you within Rs 3,000. Don't worry."

"Can you?" said the elated customer. "When can I get it?'

"One moment please," said the salesman. Soon he hurried out. When he was out of earshot, he took out his cell phone, rang up his friend and asked, "Arey Ashok, I have struck a deal at Rs 3,000 for a Pekingese, and the customer is waiting for its delivery with ready cash. But what's this bloody Pekingese?"

Conclusion

The situations discussed in this chapter are only illustrative of the usefulness and versatility of Humor. These are not exhaustive. You can harness Humor to a lot more situations depending on your preparedness, creativity, and perspective. As Patrick McManus has said, "Its never quite so funny, as when your situation is almost hopeless!"

Chapter 8

The Darker Side of Humor

"Men ought to find the difference between saltness and bitterness. Certainly, he that hath a satirical vein, as he maketh others afraid of his wit, so he had need be afraid of others' memory."

—Francis Bacon

Improper Humor

As you already know by now, Humor is a very potent communication tool. Whenever anything powerful is in your hands, it is absolutely essential that you exercise caution and care while using it. Many people are tempted to use Humor as a weapon rather than as a tool kit. In such cases Humor can seriously hurt someone. Another important point to be noted is that Humor can be misused and abused by you, inadvertently, and at times even without your knowledge. You can be in for a shock to learn that while your intended purpose of using Humor was to highlight and improve your message, the same Humor embarrassed some members of the audience. You must remember that you are not granted any license to lash out, censure, or condemn any or all the members of your audience. It's best that you banish all offensive Humor from your talk, however attractive it may look to you. The point that your Humor may be offensive and that is not always obvious to you, cannot be overemphasized. Even Humor experts often fall into the trap; this may be appreciated by the following incident.

Malcolm Kushner, the famous exponent of business Humor has narrated an experience of his which took place when he was invited by the Rotary Club, San Diego, USA, to address a gathering of nearly a thousand people, who were celebrating Valentine's Day. At the gathering, Kushner had planned to use the story about the error-prone florist who, by mistake, interchanged the floral arrangements ordered by two customers. As the story goes, the floral arrangement which was to be delivered at a funeral was handed over at the office inauguration festivity and vice versa! When Kushner reached the Rotary club, he was introduced by the Club president to a lady who had borne all the expenses of the floral decorations in the mammoth hall. It also turned out that she happened to be the widow of a recently deceased local florist. Kushner thanked his stars for this piece of timely information, for he would have seriously hurt the lady's feelings as well as of the organizers with the story he had planned to narrate and wouldn't have even known about it. So Kushner has a very valid point when he recommends to all speakers that extra care should be taken to avoid hasty and groundless assumptions about the audience.

Your Attitude

After collecting the maximum information about your audience, your next step would be to look inward at yourself. Analyze your own attitude while selecting the pieces of Humor for your presentation. In a number of cases, you'll see that your personal ego plays a very major role. It could be that you have an urge to settle an unfinished score with someone in the audience. In this case, there may be a dash of vengefulness lurking in your mind when you're blending Humor into your talk. Or, you could be keen on proving your superiority conclusively. Remember that all these approaches are not only wrong, but also dangerous. You cannot estimate the harm you inflict on yourself through these approaches.

You can insure yourself against most of these dangers staying cheerful, jovial, and amused. When you have this attitude of entertaining your listeners while communicating your message, your listeners are more tolerant, and hence do not take offence so quickly.

Let us now look at the different forms which offensive Humor can take.

Stupid Humor

This is the type of Humor usually employed by clowns in the circus. It includes making faces like Mr Bean, a man imitating a woman (or vice versa) in dress, gait, voice, gestures like walking on heels, entering the stage topsy-turvy etc., are some such physical gimmicks. These have no place in a business speaker's presentation and should be totally avoided. Such Humor may generate laughter but it would be in bad taste. It disparages the audience and in turn denigrates the speaker.

Wanton Humor

This Humor involves using a joke or some other piece of Humor to offend and humiliate an individual or group, by making fun of the latter's real or imagined weakness. With this Humor the speaker may generate plenty of laughter from a few in the audience, but he is bound to embarrass the majority. More importantly, such Humor is a sure distraction from the purpose of the speaker. You can use such Humor only if you want to display your recklessness. Some examples of this type are given ahead. (The first two are by Milton Berle.)

☺ *Our next speaker is a fine man; it's hard to exaggerate his accomplishments. But I'll do my best!*

☺ *Our next speaker will not bore you with a long speech—he can do it with a shorter one!*

☺ *The other day Mr X retired from his job; and nobody knew!*

☺ *The one thing I like about my boss's egoism is that he never talks about other people. Only himself!*

☺ *I'd like to say something nice about Mr X, but I can't think of anything!*

Pompous Humor

The speaker who uses this type of Humor is actually trying to say that he/she is a lot worthier than anyone in the audience, and is keen to see that the audience takes note of it. There may also be a dash of hostility in the speaker's attitude; like any other type of insipid Humor, this too may succeed in generating some laughter, but it is more likely to alienate the majority of listeners. And it works against you as far as your presentation is concerned. Some examples are:

☺ *The boss called in one of his assistants and shouted, "I've been told that you went to the Ganapathi temple and prayed for a promotion. How dare you go over my head?"*

☺ *In a speech to the House of Commons, Winston Churchill spoke of the then treasurer, Ramsay MacDonald: "I remember when I was a child, being taken to the celebrated Barnum's circus; there was a display of malformed persons inclusive of what was publicized as 'The Boneless Wonder.' I was somehow fascinated by this exhibit and was deeply disappointed when my parents didn't allow me to see it thinking that it would be too sickening a sight to be seen by a young boy. Since then I have been waiting for more than 50 years to see 'The Boneless Wonder' now sitting on the Treasury Bench!"*

☺ *Theodore Roosevelt (26th US President, 1901–09) while talking about his predecessor, William McKinley, said, "He has no more backbone than a chocolate eclair!" and, "He has his ear so close to the ground that it is full of grasshoppers!"*

☺ *Ronald Reagan on his predecessor Jimmy Carter:*

"A recession is when your neighbour is out of work; a depression is when you're out of work. But a recovery is when Carter is out of work!"

"Carter was once supposed to go on the TV Programme '60 Minutes', to talk about his accomplishments; but that left him with 59 minutes to fill!"

☺ *Harry Truman on Richard Nixon: "He is one of the few men in the history of America to run for the highest office, talking out of both sides of his mouth at the same time, and lying out of both sides!"*

☺ *Ronald Reagan on Jimmy Carter: "Carter said he'd do something about unemployment; he did. In April, 825,000 Americans lost their jobs!"*

☺ *A manager reached home sullen and tired. His wife received him affectionately and asked why he had such a long face. "What should I say? My boss has become a mighty problem. He's so nasty with me; but I have to say that he's also just."*

"Why do you say that?" asked the wife.

"Well, he's nasty with everybody!"

☺ *Once, two famous doctors were introduced to each other at a social gathering. They happened to be from different schools of medicine—one from alopathy and the other, homeopathy. The first one said loudly to the other while shaking his hand, "I'm glad to meet you as a gentleman, sir, though I can't admit that you're a physician".*

"And I," said the homeopath, "am glad to meet you as a physician, but I won't admit that you're a gentleman!"

Ironical Humor

This is one more hazardous form of Humor; in fact, it may be totally wrong to call it Humor because it is, to put it simply, bitterness and contempt cloaked in some wit. You're not using this Humor to highlight your message, but rather to spit contempt and disdain at the listeners. Your only gain here would be the hostility and dislike of your audience, toward you and your message. For example:

☺ *He had an extremely high IQ when he was five years old. Too bad he grew out of it!"*

☺ *"Are you trying to make a fool of me?"*

"No chance. How can I interfere in nature's work, which is already completed!"

—Milton Berle

☺ *"She has the answer to everything and solution to nothing!"*

☺ *Photographer to a group of people: "Look pleasant please; as soon as I snap this picture, you may resume your natural expressions!"*

☺ *Boss to his assistant: "Well Gopi, are you part of the problem or are you part of the solution? Decide quickly."*

Vulgar Humor

Some speakers make explicit use of improper, lewd, and erotic matter as the material for their Humor. They may, in this process, succeed in generating some laughter, but the more likely reaction of the audience would be shock, embarrassment, and disappointment. You are advised to stay far away from this form of Humor even if the other speakers sharing your platform indulge in it. Following are a few examples.

☺ *"Gopi, why do you look so worried?"*
"You don't know my problem. Yesterday, I received a phone call from some fellow warning me not to meet his wife anymore. Otherwise he said he'd kill me."
"So what? Just keep away from her."
"You don't understand; the call was made from a public booth and he didn't tell me who he was!"

☺ *A multimillionaire business magnate handed over the reins of his business empire to his young son. The new owner was very confused on his first day at his new post. He later said to a friend of his, "I felt like the son of an oil sheikh who has received a gift of a hundred of his father's concubines, who said, 'I knew what was to be done but didn't know where to begin.'"*

☺ *A Bishop was speaking with some feeling about the use of cosmetics by girls. "The more experience I have of lipstick," he declared, "the more distasteful I find it!"*

Dispelling Improper Humor

Inappropriate Humor at the workplace hurts people badly. Hence, you as a manager are duty-bound to eliminate any such Humor. Sometimes, in any group of persons, there can be tacit concensus that the group members can indulge to a certain extent in Humor which is improper, but outside the group. The type of such "accepted" Humor and its degree varies from one group to another and also from time to time. So the manager's role in dispelling improper Humor becomes tricky and the process, quite complex. Ignoring improper Humor at the workplace frustrates the victims and gradually adversely affects the work atmosphere; it is always wiser to nip it in the bud. You as a manager can discourage the person/s using poor Humor in the following ways:

(1) By not laughing.
(2) By confronting them with the question: "Can you not refrain from hurting the feelings of others"
(3) By drawing the attention of the persons to the fact that their Humor was in poor taste and that if they do not mend their ways, they will have to face disciplinary action.

One manager chose to be innovative in the way he put an end to improper Humor in his department. He said to the guy, "Your joke is very good. I will send it for inclusion in the monthly bulletin in your name."

Conclusion

Humor is a very powerful tool. There are many chances of your misusing and abusing it—intentionally or unintentionally—with the result being serious injuries to the victims. Sarcasm, ridicule, irony, satire, vulgarity, and jealousy are the causes of a number of forms of improper Humor. A few precautions, meticulously observed by you, will prevent anyone from getting hurt.

Chapter 9

The Humor Menu Card

"Good Humor is a tonic for mind and body. It is the best antidote for anxiety and depression. It is a business asset."

—Glenville Kleiser

The most common forms of Humor are jokes, stories, and anecdotes. These have been discussed in detail in the earlier chapters. This chapter is devoted to the other less common but equally effective forms of Humor, all of which can serve your purpose very eloquently. You can be discerning in your choice of Humor, depending upon the application at hand.

Quotations

Quotations are wise, weighty, and witty thoughts contributed by eminent persons from every walk of life. They are readily available on an amazingly wide range of topics from ability and absurdity to zing and zeal. When they are used to either introduce or reinforce your points, they make a big impact on the audience. This is primarily because the words you recite are actually authored by a Kalidasa or a Shakespeare whom the listeners don't dare neglect. Like with any other type of Humor, you have to first make a preamble in your talk to establish the relevance of the quotation. In this respect quotations are just like jokes.

Some examples of famous quotes are:

☺ *"It's amazing what ordinary people can achieve, if they set out without preconceived notions."*

—Charles Kettering

☺ *"The only things which evolve by themselves in an organization, are disorder, friction and malperformance!"*

—Peter Drucker

☺ *"The happiest people are those who are too busy to notice whether they are or not!"*

—William Feather

☺ *"It's a funny thing in life—if you refuse to accept anything but the best, you very often get it!"*

—Somerset Maugham

☺ *"Money is a stupid measure of achievement, but unfortunately that is the only measure we have!"*

—Charles Steinmetz

Cartoons

Cartoons have become a part of our everyday life. Whether as a single sketch cartoon or as a series of sketches, cartoons have become the darlings of everyone, from children to old veterans. Earmark the cartoons which you like and preserve their copies for future use. You can introduce the cartoon into your presentation after the necessary relevance-building exercise. You can either show the cartoon with modified captions or describe it orally to your audience. A sketched cartoon can be more easily understood by people who may sometimes fail to catch subtle verbal jokes. Cartoons score over stories or jokes, because they use very few words as can be seen by the examples in this book.

Letters

With the onset of e-mail, cell phones, answering machines, the internet and the like, letter writing has become a forgotten routine. Yet, whenever such an occasion arises, humorous language and text can make the letter an enjoyable piece,

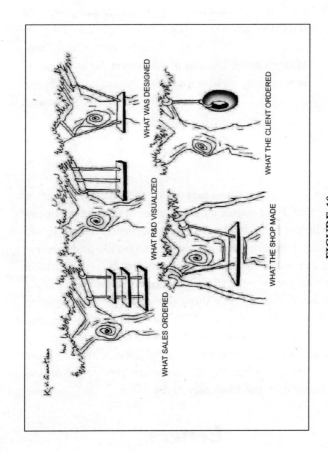

FIGURE 10

Corporate Communication Hazards

both for the sender and the receiver. A couple of letters full of wit and subtle polish are given ahead as examples to motivate you to relearn the art of humorous letter writing.

Letter A

This is a letter written by Abraham Lincoln to a friend.

"I have one vice and I can call it nothing else: it is not to be able to say 'No.' Thank God for not making me a woman, but if he had, I suppose He would have made me as ugly as He did, and no one would ever have tempted me."

Letter B

This is a letter Charles Dickens wrote to John Bennet, the owner of a clock repair shop.

"My Dear Sir:

Since my hall clock was sent to your establishment for being cleaned, it has gone (as indeed it always has) perfectly well, but has struck the hours with great reluctance, and after enduring internal agonies of a most distressing nature, it has now ceased altogether. Though a happy release for the clock, this is not convenient to the household. If you can send down any confidential person with whom the clock can confer, I think that it may have something on its works that it would be glad to make a clean breast of.

Faithfully yours,

Charles Dickens."

Letter C

Mark Twain used to receive a very large number of photographs from persons who thought that they looked like Twain.

The humorist had a standard letter of acknowledgement which he sent to such persons.

> *"My Dear Sir,*
>   *I thank you very much for your letter and photograph. In my opinion you are more like me than any of my numerous doubles. I may even say that you resemble me more than I myself do. In fact, I intend to use your picture to shave by.*
> *Yours faithfully,*
> *Mark Twain."*

Rolls

You are familiar with this funny adage: "You can get a thing done in three ways:

(a) Doing it yourself.
(b) Telling some other person to do it.
(c) Telling your children not to do it!"

—Monta Crane

Don't you feel like laughing when you read the third alternative? Okay, you felt like laughing! The first two alternatives suggested herein make you believe that the third one will be along similar lines and hence you are filled with shock and surprise to hear an unexpected type of suggestion in the third alternative. Such a piece of Humor, which is called a Roll, will have three or more items in series. The items other than the last are aimed at misguiding your expectation, while the last one is meant to trigger the mental explosion. Rolls call for a higher degree of mental application to conceive and draw up.

Some examples are as follows.

The Secret

Follow three principles to have healthy teeth:

(a) *brush them after each meal;*
(b) *drink plenty of cow's milk; and*
(c) *never poke your nose into others' business!*

Three Types of Clients

A celebrated lawyer said that his three most troublesome clients were:

(a) *a young lady who wanted to marry;*
(b) *a married woman who wanted a divorce; and*
(c) *an old maid who didn't know what she wanted!*

Advice to Managers

(a) *When in charge, ponder;*
(b) *when in trouble, delegate; and*
(c) *when in doubt, mumble!"*

—James H. Boren

Formula for Success

Try:

(a) *aspiration;*
(b) *inspiration; and*
(c) *perspiration!*

Insults

"The only graceful way to handle an insult is to ignore it; if you can't ignore it, top it; if you can't top it, laugh at it; if you can't laugh at it, you deserve it!"

—J. Russel Lynes

Forgetting

"First you forget names, then you forget faces, then you forget to pull your zipper up, and then you forget to pull your zipper down!"

Technology

"There are three roads to ruin. Women, gambling and technology. The most pleasant is with the women; the quickest is with gambling; but the surest is with Technology."

—Georges Pompidou

Similes and Exaggerations

A simile is exactly the figure of speech you had learnt in your grammar class in high school; it is a comparison. But here, for purposes of Humor, the comparison is between something very routine with something superlative or absurd.

An exaggeration is an intentional overstatement to cause fun.

Both these devices are sure to draw the attention of the listeners and make your words memorable.

Similes

☺ *"Trying to get information from that lady at the counter is like trying to suck a bowling ball through a 10 m rubber hose pipe!"*

☺ *"Commissioning a management information system is like mating elephants. It's done at a really high level and there's a lot of bellowing!"*

☺ *"I have two types of speeches. First, there is the Mother Hubbard speech, which like her garment covers everything but doesn't touch anything. Then there is the French Bikini speech which touches the vital points and leaves the rest uncovered."*

☺ *"Sometimes I feel like the young boy who, when he received a huge Alsatian dog as his birthday gift from his parents, asked, 'Is he for me, or am I for him?'"*

☺ *"A new idea is just like a baby—easier conceived than delivered!"*

☺ *Once a very thin man started boring Douglas Jerrold, the famous comedian. Finally, Douglas told the fellow, "Sir, you're like a pin, but without either the head or the point!"*

Exaggeration:

☺ *"I have a feeling that my house isn't too strong. The other day, I saw termites wearing helmets!"*

—Milton Berle

☺ *A government official had a sign on his desk which read: This job of mine is so secret, the I don't know what I'm doing!*

Deft Definitions

Deft definitions are the products of ingenuity. A routine word which is a part of the presentation title or of a question

FIGURE 11
Two Types of Speeches

or a statement is selected and then explained to have a funny meaning. This is possible by looking at a common thing in an uncommon way with the end result being a lot of fun. Let's look at some examples.

- ☺ *Public Speaking: This is the art of expressing a two-minute idea with a two-hour vocabulary!*
- ☺ *Management: It consists of making it difficult for people to work!*
- ☺ *Pessimist: Someone who can look at the land of milk and honey and see only calories and cholesterol!*
- ☺ *Bankruptcy: It is a legitimate practice of keeping your money in your trousers and handing over your jacket to the bankers!*
- ☺ *Bad Motorist: Someone who keeps the poor pedestrians in good running condition!*
- ☺ *Ambassador: One who having failed to secure an office from the people, is given one by the government on condition that he leaves the country!*

Acronyms

Perhaps you may remember your first ever acronym from your geometry class days. The proof of every theorem used to have the letters "QED" at the bottom. Our teacher explained that the letters stood for the Latin word which meant "That which was to be proved." We students would translate it as:

QED = Quite easily done.

An acronym as you have by now understood is the shortened form of a group of words. While the conventional meaning could be an ordinary phrase, you as a humorist can attribute it a new funny meaning. Some examples are given here. You are advised to scout for more and create new ones of your own.

- ☺ *TQM (Total Quality Management): you could instead explain it as "Thoroughly Questionable Management!"*
- ☺ *JIT (Just in Time): You could explain it as "Junk in Transit!"*
- ☺ *ASAP (As soon as possible): You could explain it as "All Supervisors are Panicky!" or "As Silly as Possible!"*
- ☺ *PTO (Please Turn Over): This could be explained as "Please Throw Out!"*
- ☺ *TOT (Time on Target): It could be "Trouble over Terminal!"*
- ☺ *SOP (Standard Operating Procedure): This could be "Share our Pizza!"*
- ☺ *DOB (Date of Birth): This could be "Devilish Old Boss!"*
- ☺ *AT&T (All Theft and Thuggery!): This could be "Always Tired and Tipsy!"*

Observations

Observations are funny remarks or expressions made by people like you and me. Generally, they are short, witty, and can be used by almost anyone. A number of them explain the absurdities which have crept into our daily routines. The observer takes a step back from the scene, becomes somewhat detached or neutral from the active members, and then looks at things. See some of the examples given ahead and create your own collection.

☺ *"The guy who invented spray paint must have got the idea when he sneezed while drinking tomato juice!"*

—Pat Williams

☺ *"If the customer who owes you part of last year's coal bill springs a new television aerial, somebody is a better salesman than you are!"*

☺ *"If you grudge paying all your bills at the end of the month, there is an easy way out; pay at the beginning!"*

☺ *"Mirrors reflect without speaking; while women speak without reflecting!"*

☺ *"There are two reasons why some people don't mind their own business: one is they don't have any business, and the other, they don't have any mind!"*

—Roy Zuck

☺ *"Learning to drive a car and learning to play golf are both not so easy. But there is one difference; when you learn golf you don't hit anything!"*

☺ *"A man is an irrational creature; he looks for home atmosphere in a hotel and a hotel like atmosphere around the house!"*

☺ *"My boss and I are on very good terms. I laugh whenever he jokes and he laughs whenever I make any suggestions!"*

—Pat Williams

Euphemisms

Euphemisms are polite, peaceful, and tranquilizing substitute words used to express a grave situation; they are the disguise employed when you find it embarrassing to speak the truth. When you have to break bad news but want to cushion the blow, euphemisms come in very handy.

The world of Humor employs euphemisms to amuse even in such tricky situations. They bring appreciation from listeners, because euphemisms reflect the concern shown and pains taken to lessen the shock of any bad news. Euphemisms are also used in the "The good news is ... and the bad news is ..." form to fulfil the same purpose. See some of the following examples.

☺ *The chairman and managing director was addressing the shareholders at the AGM after a disastrous annual performance.*

"Respected shareholders, you may remember that in the last AGM I had stated that our company was on the brink of collapse. This year you may note that we've taken one step forward!"

☺ *Hollywood actor: "My wife and I were happy for 20 years. Then we met!"*

☺ *A speaker paused during his speech and asked the chairman if he was making a bore of himself. The chairman replied: "Well Sir, I would put it this way—you never seem to have an unexpressed thought!"*

☺ *Old age can get consolation from hearing the following description: "Tempestuous twenties, terrible thirties, ferocious forties, fearful fifties, satisfied sixties, serene seventies, ethical eighties and noble nineties."*

Euphemism in Management Jargon

Following are some examples of euphemisms in management.

(1) "That's very interesting" means "I disagree!"
(2) "We have an opportunity" means "we have a problem!"

(3) "Your project is on hold" means "forget about your project!"

(4) "To expedite" means "To confound confusion!"

(5) "Company policy" means "Request not granted!"

Euphemisms of the Good News/Bad News Form

☺ *A vice president, finance, reporting to CEO, said, "Sir, the bad news is, in the recent acquisition frenzy, we purchased one of our own companies; the good news is that the stock went up."*

☺ *"The world is moving from bad to worse" was the summary of the survey report submitted to God, who had sent his staff to collect information about the latest situation on Earth. So, God reluctantly came to the decision to end all life on the planet. He called the three most powerful people on Earth: George Bush, the President of USA; Hu Jintao, the President of the People's Republic of China; and Jeffrey R. Immelt, the Chairman and CEO of General Electric Co. Inc. God briefed them on the highlights of the survey and about his decision to end the world; he asked them to go back and inform mankind about this.*

The White House organized a worldwide live TV broadcast on which Bush declared that he had good news and bad news; the good news was that Americans now need not worry about either Osama Bin Laden or Iraq; the bad news was that the world would be ending very soon.

The Chinese President called a meeting of the officeholders of the Communist Party of China and announced that he had bad news and good news. The bad news was that there was God whose presence had been always denied by their party and the good news was that as the world was anyway going to end shortly; they did not need to worship that God.

The Chairman of GE called a special general body meeting of all the shareholders and announced that he had good news and better news. The good news was that as the world was going to end shortly, henceforth the company need not worry about the environmental scandals it had been facing; the better news was that even God acknowledged that their company was so highly influential, that he had invited its chairman for a confidential meeting.

Improvisations

There are occasions when even an experienced speaker, in spite of his elaborate planning and preparation, makes some slips when he gets up and starts his speech. Great speakers immediately correct themselves by using a humorous remark, even about their error, thereby converting what was a potentially negative situation into one which gains audience applause. This technique also comes in handy when something adverse occurs suddenly, like the lights going off, the microphone failing, a background noise shooting up, etc. These remarks to improvise the situation should appear to be natural and spontaneous; hence most well-known speakers are usually well prepared. They anticipate most of the things which can go wrong and keep ready a couple of witty remarks for any eventuality. Observe the following examples.

☺ **If the microphone fails,** *you can say, "This microphone reminds me of my wife; it is not giving me any chance to speak!"*

☺ **If the lights go out,** *you can say, "Why do I have a feeling that when the lights come back, I'll be alone?"*

—Pat Williams

☺ **If you forget something,** *you can say, "Where was I? Oh, Yes! I was here!" (Take a step to the side while doing so.) Or, "This is terrible; every year Maruti Motors recall more and more and I'm recalling less and less!"*

☺ **If your slide is upside down,** *you can say, "It looks good, no matter how you look at it!" Or, "For those of you standing on your heads!"*

☺ **If someone points out a spelling mistake in your slide,** *you can say, "Mark Twain said that he never respected anyone who couldn't spell a word more than one way!"*

☺ **If someone gets up to leave,** *you can say, "Now you know why they call me a motivational speaker!"*

—Pat Williams

☺ **To inviting the audience to applaud,** *you can say, "I'll make a deal. I'll stop talking when you start applauding!"*

—Pat Williams

☺ **For inviting questions,** *you can say, "Don't hesitate to ask the simplest and most basic questions, because that's the only kind of questions I can answer!"*

—Pat Williams

Conclusion

The 10 tasty dishes included in the Humor menu card are sure to tickle your Humor taste buds. These along with the varieties of jokes, stories, general anecdotes, and personal anecdotes discussed earlier provide you with a rich variety of Humor; even though I would hasten to emphasize that this would not mean an exhaustive list. Once you master these varieties, you would have progressed so much that you will easily recognize additional varieties of Humor as and when you come across them; these can be added to your stock of Humor. The secret of gaining expertise in any form of Humor lies in using it as frequently as possible and vigilantly observing whenever others use it.

Chapter 10

The Armor of Humor

"Humor is just another defence against the universe."
—Mel Brooks

Have you ever come across people who have charisma? I would prefer the term used by Malcolm Kushner "Armor of Humor." We may find it difficult to describe this quality completely, even though it is very easy to recognize a person who is gifted with this rare quality. A person who wears this "Armor of Humor" has a distinctive allure and can create an excellent rapport with the people he wants to contact. Such a person can enter a meeting hall, full of people at loggerheads with one another, and using only a few words can magically create camaraderie; he can inspire the same people to team up and achieve lofty goals. He can set challenging tasks for his people and can insist on superhuman efforts without appearing to be harsh or nasty. He can exhibit very fine Humor even in the face of catastrophe, dispelling the gloom which darkens the minds of his people. Self-deprecating Humor comes so naturally to him that he can mix with his people very easily. It is small wonder that such a person stands very tall in any group and is a valuable asset to his organization.

This chapter aims at providing guidelines for you to acquire such an Armor of Humor. However, the major role has to be played by you. You have to take complete charge and be open to changes and improvements. Be assured that the rewards you get are so bountiful and self-fulfilling that you will have no regrets.

Humor Relieves Stress and Relaxes You

Among the many benefits that you can gain from Humor, I would rank as number one its amazing potential to relieve stress and provide relaxation. Stress is recognized as the disease of this century and its ill effects are seen growing larger and larger.

Norman Vincent Peale, the well-known proponent of positive living, laments that America has become too tense and nervous and that it has been years since he has seen anyone asleep in church, and that is a sad situation.

The situation is no better in the other countries of the world. Generally, stress is caused by exaggerated fear. You fear the unknown by imagining the worst, like the young girl who saw a shark movie on TV and later went along with her parents to a seaside resort during the holidays. She was thrilled at the sight of the sand and sea and wanted to go into the water. But she remembered the shark in the movie and was scared stiff. Her father held her hand reassuringly and said, "Look here, Meera," said he, "there are more people killing sharks in this world, than sharks killing people. So it is the sharks which are afraid of people." These words dispelled the girl's fears and she had a nice time enjoying the surf and the sea.

Draw up a Stress Scale

It is very similar in your case. You have developed a habit of feeling disproportionately high fear even over minor troubles. You do realize this, usually after second thoughts or after some passage of time. You should therefore learn to differentiate between the real tragedies and the apparent ones. You can do this if you have a measuring system which has marks at its two extremities: the greatest tragedy marked 10 at the top and the lowest discomfort marked 1 at the bottom, thereby allowing you to fit in all the possible mishaps you may face in between. This technique is recommended by Bob Ross, author of the book *That's a Good One!* So when you face trouble next time, instead of pressing the panic button directly, you can compare the situation with those you have ranked in your system and recognize the gravity of the situation accurately. This step will control your fear and limit the intensity of stress you experience. The scale given here is to help illustrate the principle. You can prepare a scale most suitable for your situation and make full use of that to your advantage.

TABLE 1: Stress Scale

Model Stress Scale		Your Stress Scale
10	Terminal Disease/Stroke	10
9	Permanent Disability	9
8	Loss of Income Source	8
7	Chronic Disease	7
6	Death/Terminal Disease of close family member	6
5	Disablement of close family member	5
4	Heavy Financial Loss	4
3	Facing Imprisonment	3
2	Family Dissensions	2
1	Temporary Ill Health	1

During my visit to San Jose I was staying with my nephew Ramu for about a week. Once while driving, Ramu pulled up at a traffic signal; his BMW started vibrating. He looked very worried. I remarked that we were experiencing an earthquake. Ramu readily agreed and instantly looked extremely relieved. He exclaimed, "Thank God, I was afraid that the car was in trouble!"

Make a List of 'Important' Subjects

This exercise is recommended by Annette Goodheart, the famous author of *Laughter Therapy*. When you make a list of all the subjects you currently consider as important, you will realize the endlessness of the interests you are engaged in, each of which has a potential to cause stress, if left as it is. This realization is sure to change your attitude toward your interests. You are more likely to conclude that it is impossible to have so many "important" interests. You would laugh about most of them and proceed to cancel them from the list. So make this list regularly, at least once a year.

Laugh More, Smile More

Laughter is the joy of all joys, so laugh as much as possible. Initially, you may have to force it, but gradually you will graduate from mild laughter to genuine laughter. If laughing seems troublesome, opt for smiling from ear to ear instead. You will be surprised to see that smiling leads you to laughter.

Collect Toys

Adults need toys more than children. You should buy toys and keep some on your desk. Your colleagues, when they come to you, will set the toys into play; you may also join in. Notice how toys enable you to laugh freely without any specific reason; they make you less priggish. In addition, toys at the workplace can remove any tension that may be generated during discussions or arguments. So visit a toy store and buy toys like a wading duck, jumping monkey, chirping parrot, a teddy bear, a bouncing ball, etc., and enjoy their usefulness.

Play with Puppies

Play with young puppies or kittens or any other domesticated animals and you will realize what great fun it is. Do you remember the TV ad for Raymond suitings, which showed a man in a suit being welcomed home by a litter of white puppies? It was a scene of unique enjoyment.

Find Friends Who Can Laugh

Check the number of times you laugh in a day that is spent with the people whom you meet regularly. You will observe that there are very few occasions of laughter. You therefore have to regularly meet other people and explore opportunities to laugh. Identify the people with whom you can laugh most and meet them frequently.

Admire Someone

Psychologists say that most of our conversations include criticizing others; admiration and applause for another is very rare. It is not easy for us to either give compliments or receive them. You should make it a point to admire someone or the other from time to time. Your admiration should look genuine and natural. Practice will make things easy.

Exercise Laughter

Join a laughter club in your locality. Become a regular and active member. If this is not possible, take a little time everyday to laugh a couple of minutes.

Repeat:

I am Humorous ... Ha, Ha, Ho, Ho.

I am Creative ... Ha, Ha, Ho, Ho, Ha, Ha, Ha, Ha, Ho, Ho, Ho, Ho!

Create Your FUN FILE

Take out a new file and name it "Fun File". Whenever you come across funny stories, jokes, anecdotes, cartoons, photographs, news bits, communications, make copies of these and preserve them in this file. Whenever you feel depressed, glance through this file. Whenever you are in need of a Humor piece to garnish your talk, presentation, or conversation, look through this file. Keep on adding to this file whenever you find something amusing. Always keep a paper and pen handy so whenever you come across something humorous, you can record it for later addition in your Fun File.

Have Fun with Cartoons

Cartoons can provide fun to almost everyone, and you can derive much more amusement by this exercise. Cut out the cartoons you like from their source. Take out the title and the text. Think about the funniest way of using the cartoon to depict your work situation and add a new title and text to bring out your funny thought. You can improve the captions to attribute the cartoon to your colleagues, boss, etc. Repeat this with some more cartoons to have more fun.

Create New Laws

The law is something which you have always tried to adhere to, though sometimes you were not very happy doing so. How do you feel when your Sense of Humor empowers you to formulate new laws? The only difference is that the law of the legal world is formulated first and then adhered to, whereas the law defined by you is acted upon by people first and then formulated.

The latter variety helps you in keeping your cool in annoying situations, because they offer very logical and amusing justifications. Some such well-known laws are:

Parkinson's Law:	Work expands so as to fill the time for completion!
Peter's Law:	In a hierarchy, every employee tends to rise to his level of incompetence!
Murphy's Law:	Anything that can go wrong, will go wrong!
Billing's Law:	Live within your income, even if you have to borrow to do so!

Gate's Law:	If there isn't a law, there will be!
Truman's Law:	If you can't convince him, confuse him!

These law enunciators have faced troublesome situations in life and because of their Sense of Humor they have laughed at them. So the next time when you face some difficulty, you can think about which law describes the situation best. If there isn't one, you can formulate one and can have the privilege of giving your name to it. See some more examples given below.

Gresham's Law:	Bad money will drive out good money!
Lewis Law:	No matter how long or how hard you may shop for an item, immediately after you've bought it, it will be on sale somewhere, cheaper!
Anthony's Law:	Any tool, when dropped, will roll into the least accessible corner of the workshop, and on the way to the corner, any dropped tool will first strike your toes!
Kaufmann's Paradox:	The less important you are to the corporation, the more your tardiness or absence is noticed!
Miller's Law:	An insurance policy covers everything except what happens!

Lampner's Law: When you leave work late, you'll go unnoticed; when leaving early, you'll meet the boss at the main entrance!

If you can recall your school days, you may agree that the following laws were operative, but you weren't aware of them:

(1) The tests which you didn't attend were the easiest!
(2) On the day of the school trip, you were ill!
(3) Whenever you forgot a book, you were asked to read!
(4) Whenever you had completed the arithmetic home-work, the arithmetic teacher would be on leave!

Titles

Make a list of the people who interact with you regularly. Take into account the usual topics of discussion between you and them; also take into account their attitudes toward you. Allot to each of these people a title which could be the name of a movie or serial. The title would describe the person in an amusing manner. For example, one of your colleagues talks very sweetly to you but goes on complaining to the boss against you, you can call him, "Cloak and Dagger." Or your boss and the chief of marketing do not get on well and this makes your life in the production division difficult. Whenever the two meet, it is with daggers drawn you assign them the title "Komodo vs Cobra". Our final example is of the accounts manager who constantly raises objections to your travel expense reports and therefore deserves to be called "Barbwire." There can be many more such cases where you can think up funny titles.

Proverbs

Every country has a number of proverbs in usage and these can serve as fertile ground for you to create your own Humor by building on them to suit today's situations. Collect as many proverbs as you can from all available resources, including your memory. Try fiddling around with one of them to make it sound funny as well as apt, under current conditions.

Following are a few examples:

1. *Early to bed and early to rise, makes a man, healthy, wealthy and wise.*
   Changed form:
   Early to bed and early to rise, makes a man boring!
2. *To err is human.*
   Changed form:
   To err is human; but to make a real mess of things, you need a computer!
3. *Never put off till tomorrow, what you can do today.*
   Changed form:
   Never put off till tomorrow, what can be totally avoided!
4. *He who laughs last, laughs the loudest.*
   Changed form:
   He who laughs last is the last one to get the joke!

5. *A friend in need is a friend indeed.*
   Changed forms:
   A friend in need is to be totally avoided!
   A friend who is not in need is a friend indeed!
6. *An apple a day keeps the doctor away.*
   Changed form:
   A garlic a day keeps everyone away!

Definitions

Many speakers try to explain the topic of their discussion by giving the dictionary meanings of the topic and elucidating them further. A very humorous alternative is to attribute a funny interpretation of the words involved and then returning to the agenda. You can also use this technique to counter any adverse comments on the point you are making.

For example, if you make a presentation about a new product line and declare the line to have a very good revenue potential and someone in the group quotes certain statistical data to counter your claim, you can say, "Statistics? Statistics can be very misleading. You know, statistics tell you that when you have one leg in ice and the other in boiling water, you are comfortable. Who interprets statistics? *A Statistician* is a person who does not have the personality to become an accountant!"

Some more definitions are given ahead. You can search for more and create your own collection.

| *Acquaintance:* | A person whom we know very well when we have to borrow, and not so well when we are asked to lend. |

Economist:	An expert who will know tomorrow why the things he predicted yesterday did not happen today!
Programmer:	One who solves a problem you didn't know you had, in a way you don't understand.
Husband:	A person who thinks he bosses the house but in reality houses the boss!
Economy:	Means the large size in toothpaste and the small size in automobiles!
Maintenance-free:	That which when broken cannot be repaired!
Lawyer:	One who writes a 10,000 word document and calls it a "brief!"

Revelations or Gems of Common Sense

Common sense is generally uncommon. You come across many wise sayings and adages which hold out great sense compacted into the fewest of words. They can be epigrams, mottos, proverbs, or witty remarks. They are valuable in any communication and help support your arguments and embellish your language. You can draft, on your own, such revelations and enjoy sharing them with others. These maxims will bring out your ability to take a balanced view of all that is happening around you, with a detached perspective. This is a very powerful technique to highlight the silly, unreasonable, and senseless things which happen without hurting anyone too much. See some of the following examples.

1. *Wrong is wrong, even if everyone does it!*
2. *If you don't have time to do it right, you'll be forced to find time to do it twice or thrice over!*
3. *The only thing worse than an expert is someone who thinks he is an expert!*
4. *The greatest undeveloped territory in the world lies under our hat!*
5. *If you think your boss is stupid, remember you wouldn't have had your job had he been smarter!*

—Albert Grant

6. *We confess our little faults to suggest that we have no big ones!*

—La Ro Chefoucauld

7. *The trouble with this world is that the stupid are cocksure, and the wise are full of doubts!*

—Betrand Russell

8. *Life is rainbow—it needs both downpours and sunshine to create the colors!*
9. *There is nothing in this world which is totally wrong; even a dead timepiece shows correct time twice a day!*
10. *There are only two ways of getting on in this world: by one's own industry or by the stupidity of others!*

—Jean de la Bruyere

Creative Visualization

Many successful and famous people have used the concept of creative visualization, right from the time they planned their strategy of attaining their life goals. It is said that Jim Carrey, the famous comedian, years before he had a break-through in his career, told himself, "I am one of the top five actors. Every director wants to work with me." Not only that, he wrote himself a cheque in which he had written, "For acting services rendered, $10 million."

Creative visualization is the technique of using your imagination to see the goal you are aiming at, in the achieved condition. Your reminding yourself regularly of the prospective outcome of reaching the goal, keeps you constantly creative and motivated. If you're planning to use a few Humor pieces in your presentation; imagine a scenario where your presentation is met with great success. Like Jim Carrey, visualize yourself as "Numero Uno" and prepare. Such an approach is bound to give positive results. This ability to visualize will be highly helpful in another kind of situation too. Imagine yourself listening to someone else reciting an anecdote or a joke in his presentation and the joke falling flat. Your visualization will enable you to imagine the scene ending differently had the joke succeeded, and this in turn will enable you to determine the changes which will improve the presentation. So, by visualizing creatively you will be actively learning out of the mistakes of others.

The Thing I Like About...

It is well known that you cannot expect to have a full glass of milk always. There are some situations which are harsh, some people who are nasty, and some events which are very distressing. However, your Sense of Humor enables you to recognize "The thing I like about..." in such persons, events, or situations, regardless of how disappointing, repulsive and traumatic they may be.

For example, "The Thing I like about adversity is that it teaches me to become creative!" To sharpen your creativity in this regard, first make a list of such unpleasant irritants you come across and then list the things you like about them. Following are some examples.

(1) *Retirement:*   "Now for doing nothing, I need not go to the office!"
(2) *Married Life:*   "After getting bored with myself when I was single, I can now get bored with someone else!"
(3) *Gossip:*   "It is something I like to hear, about someone I don't!"
(4) *Bosses:*   "I don't have to live with them!"
(5) *New Employees:*   "They cannot find my faults!"

Change Your Routine

We perform a number of our activities as a matter of routine. When we follow a routine, we do not consciously think about what we do; we are not completely aware of our acts. We would be doing something and thinking about something totally different. In order to increase your awareness, start doing routine things in different ways, in nonroutine ways. Like getting up from the other side of the bed, changing the order of putting on your inner clothing, similarly changing the order of wearing outer clothing, changing the route you take from home to the workplace etc. These changes in themselves may not be important, but they will make you start thinking of what you're doing. This will sharpen your ability to visualize and also lead you to develop a humorous perspective.

Be an Understanding Listener

Whenever we communicate with others our first priority is that others should understand us. In our haste to be understood we lose our patience while listening to others. Listening is not just hearing. If we listen carefully to others, we should be able to understand what they say verbally and even what they don't say verbally but convey through their facial expressions, body language, undulations of voice, intonation, etc. If we understand others well, we should be able to present their version of a story at least to the same effect as they do, if not more effectively. All this is possible only if we listen, not just with our ears but also with our minds.

How is listening related to Humor? Your Humor, as has been highlighted earlier, is an accessory to your communication. Unless you give priority to understanding others, why should they place importance on understanding you or your Humor? Focused, attentive listening is the cheapest and most effective way of conveying to others that you value them as important; it motivates the other people to be attracted and influenced by you.

Additionally, when you listen to others there are chances of you gaining golden nuggets of Humor. If they say something funny which makes people laugh, it can be a good addition to your collection. Then there is always unintended Humor too. Listen carefully to the discrepancies among what is said, what is meant, and what is understood. All these are freely available to you for future use; by listening you will learn how to avoid such pitfalls when you communicate.

Following are some examples of such incongruities which may be intended or inadvertent.

- ☺ *"If God had intended that Sunrise should be seen by us, would He not have made it to occur later in the day?"*
- ☺ *"You can't overestimate the unimportance of practically everything!"*
- ☺ *One girl to the other: "Well, it's true that we are having a little disagreement. I want to have a grand wedding and he wants to break off the engagement!"*
- ☺ *"Truly the times are changing. Twenty years ago, when I would leave a restaurant I would check whether I left behind anything. Now when I leave, I check if I am left with anything!"*
- ☺ *"We're going to continue having these meetings everyday, till I find out why no work is getting done!"*
- ☺ *"My uncle owns a dozen gasoline stations and not one of them has any roof because my uncle wants to avoid overheads!"*
- ☺ *Heard at a restaurant: "We've been waiting here since 40 minutes. No one has approached us to take our orders. You have converted clients into 'waiters'. Congratulations!"*

Develop a Jocular Attitude

As we grow up, we lose our playfulness and jovial attitude. We smile less frequently and forget how to laugh. Most of the times our laughter is faked. These are serious personal losses and in order to put an end to any such further loss you have to develop a jocular attitude toward life in general, and to the people and environment around you in particular.

You can start checking this attitude first on yourself. This subject has already been thoroughly discussed in Chapter 4. This is just a reminder that if you want to look at others in a humorous light you should be good at laughing at yourself first.

Make a List of "What Ifs"

In order to be able to look at the funny side of things, it is necessary that you should first stop worrying. Most of us have become natural worriers. Humor can teach you to smother worry before it grows out of proportion. While combating worry, remember two things.

1. You can only change some things, those which are in your control.
2. You have to accept things beyond your control and learn to live with them.

Remembering these two truths, list all your worries on a big sheet of paper. Scrutinize each worry separately. While scrutinizing the first one, ask yourself, "What is the worst thing that can happen? If so, what?"

Write down the answers which come to your mind against each of your worries. When you complete this step you will be surprised to see that most of your worries are minor when compared to the problems you have solved earlier. Only a few of the worries listed are important and deserve thoughtful action. The worries that are beyond your control do not deserve your attention and should simply be accepted as and when they occur.

By this exercise you gain a new perspective on yourself and your surroundings. For example, imagine your boss telling you that you may lose your current job. By adhering to the "What if" approach you can think of the following:

(a) What are all the things you can now do to retain your job?
(b) Out of the steps listed in point (a) above, which are the ones you have completed? Which are yet to be done?
(c) If all the above steps fail, what is the worst thing that can happen?
(d) How can you convert the loss of this job into an opportunity to better your career?
(e) What if you lose this job?

Humor Workshop

Conduct a Humor workshop for yourself by going through the following steps.

Step 1

Search for 12 pieces of Humor which are to *your* liking. These could be jokes, anecdotes, stories, or one-liners. They should be interesting to you to make you think that you can use them later in your communications.

This exercise will initiate you into some research and collection of useful matter. Second, it will tell you which varieties of Humor are to your liking. Further, this will sharpen your Humor selecting and collecting skills. If you carry out this exercise on a regular basis, you will be on your way to creating a large Humor library of your own.

Step 2

Write down three funny stories or jokes from your memory which you think you can use in your communications later. These should not have been covered in step 1 above. Since you will be writing these Humor pieces from your memory without referring to any book, magazine, or newspaper, they will require some work in terms of polish and power. You need not worry too much about that.

Step 3

Search for a dozen good quotations which are humorous on the following two subjects:

(1) People
(2) Money

Again, the idea is to make you collect material which you like and which you think you can use later.

Step 4

In this exercise you have to collect humorous material which you can use as possible opening lines in the following hypothetical situation.

You have been invited, as the chief guest, to inaugurate a new manufacturing facility of one of the vendors who has been regularly supplying to your company for more than a decade.

Step 5

Imagine being the boss of a group of employees who have been informed that a new system of working will be introduced from the 1st day of the coming month. The group has expressed its keenness to continue with the old system. You are now required to persuade them to accept the new system. Write down a humor piece based on any source which can serve as an effective preamble in this situation.

Step 6

This is in continuation of step 5 above. The new system has been introduced as scheduled and three months have passed since its implementation. Still, the new system has not given the expected monthly results because of a number of errors which are creeping in, mostly because of the carelessness and ignorance of the employees. You are required to deliver a message that such mistakes are proving very costly to the company; there is need for a change in the group's attitude. Prepare a Humor piece which can bolster your message in the minds of the workers. You will first put across your message in your peptalk, followed by the Humor piece to heighten the effect.

Step 7

Take one of the anecdotes or stories you used in steps 1 or 2. Think of using this in three different ways, i.e., to highlight three separate points or three forms of the story to suit three different situations.

This exercise will enable you to learn how to make your Humor versatile.

Step 8

Select three Humor pieces from steps 1 or 2 and write short introductions to these pieces to suit the situations where you think you can use them.

Step 9

Select a Humor piece from any of the exercises so far, modify it so that it can be used as a new joke or anecdote. You can change the persons, place, events mentioned in the original; you can even alter the punch line. The result should be a good, new piece of Humor.

Step 10

Create your own original Piece of Humor. You can take inspiration from any of the Humor pieces in this book and by using the trial-and-error method, make a new Piece of Humor ready for use.

Conclusion

At this stage you may perhaps think, "Well, the Armor of Humor may be very effective; but acquiring it is a Himalayan task." True, yet you need not be discouraged. Even the conquerors of the Himalayas, when they first stepped out of their homes, had the same feelings of doubt and apprehension like you. But they neither stopped nor turned back; they simply pressed forward. Likewise, keep doing the exercises detailed earlier, regularly and with perseverance. If you cannot do all of them, do as many and as often as you can. Slowly, but surely, your Humor skills will flourish. You will soon see the positive results of the blending of your Humor as a management device in effectively discharging your official schedule of responsibilities.

Chapter 11

Putting Humor on the Agenda

"Shared laughter creates a bond of friendship. When people laugh together, they cease to be young and old, teacher and pupils, worker and boss. They become a single group of human beings."
— W. Lee Grant

The preceding chapters have explained the multitude of advantages which Humor can provide when appropriately used in a business organization. By now, you have also got an insight into some of the important types of Humor which you can put into use. Therefore, it is now important that this knowledge is put into use to achieve desired results. A large number of successful business leaders have derived and are deriving very good leverage by harnessing Humor in their organizations. I am not suggesting that without Humor in your agenda, you will fail. As Jean-Louis Barsony has said, "Managers who see no need for Humor, are unlikely to fail; but they may find themselves hacking their way to the green, with a putter."

A manager who does not like to laugh may be a strong ruler, but his people will only do what he tells them and nothing more. In today's global marketplace, there is really no alternative to committed employees who use their judgement to see the larger picture, take decisions and perform far more than what they have been instructed to. Good Humor, when put on your agenda properly, plays a catalytic role in creating job satisfaction, enthusiasm, and commitment in employees. Judgement is to be used in deciding the course of action in implementing Humor in just the same way as in the application of other management techniques.

The steps detailed ahead are only suggestive and not exhaustive; nor are they all mandatory. Each organization is

FIGURE 12
Humor Your Way to Profits!

unique; even its needs for appropriate Humor. Depending on your judgement as well as the span of your jurisdiction, you may assign priority to the several steps detailed ahead. As the benefits of Humor begin to accrue, you may visualize new additions to the agenda. Many organizations have experienced an upswing in employee morale and job satisfaction after the implementation of the following steps.

A vast majority of managers, even after being convinced that Humor is a marvelous thing, hesitate to take any steps to implement Humor at their place of work. Make sure that you do not join them. As some wise person said, "There are three types of people in this world: those who make things happen; those who watch them happen; and those who wonder what happened!"

It is your privilege to make something happen right now, wherever you are.

1. When you recruit people, give preference to those with a good Sense of Humor; other qualifications and experience requirements being equal. Nancy Hauge, director of HR, Sun Microsystems, is reported to assess the candidate's Sense of Humor at the time of interview by observing the time taken by the candidate to laugh or tell something funny.

2. Clearly inform all your people that you are keen on making their work enjoyable. Before your announcement, chalk out your plan and get the approval of the top management. Also, take your immediate assistants into confidence and ensure that they fully support you in your plan.

3. After completing step 2, delegate the responsibility of implementing your Humor plan to your immediate

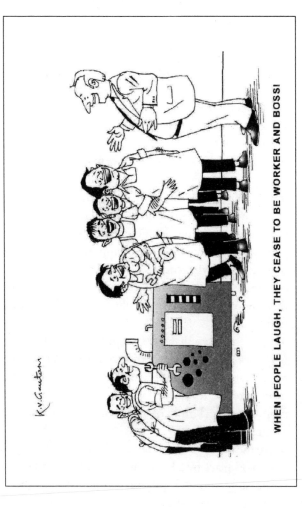

WHEN PEOPLE LAUGH, THEY CEASE TO BE WORKER AND BOSS!

FIGURE 13
Humor Knows No Barriers!

assistants and to other employees. Explain them the objectives of the plan again and again. Encourage them to take a keen interest through rewards, appreciation letters, etc., whenever their contribution is noteworthy.

4. Embellish your communications with a suitable piece of Humor and appreciate the sender whenever this step is reciprocated.

5. Display in your office (or in your office space), an appropriate amount of Humor. For example, hang a warranty certificate of your doormat.

6. Create a proper space for your employees to exhibit their products of Humor. It can be a dedicated room, or if a room is not possible, a special booth or a wall which can become the designated 'fun point' for your department. Invite the employees to fill this space by displaying their jokes, cartoons, caricatures, one-liners etc. Encourage everyone to make use of this opportunity. Some people may need repeated nudging.

7. Take steps to see that the system mentioned in step 6 grows from strength to strength. Take active interest in its progress. Encourage those who show more interest to cajole everyone else to keep on contributing. Think of novel ideas to keep the program alive.

8. Make use of personalized pictures and cartoons to suit your workplace by adding suitable captions and texts.

9. Invite suggestions from your people to help them be more creative and to make the workplace more enjoyable.

10. Display humorous messages in prominent locations; see that these messages tickle the reader apart from providing useful guidance.

11. Arrange to have an Annual Humor Program. You can organize a humorous speech, a comedy show, or have a fancy dress party.

12. Organize a departmental fun book. Include all the memorable Humor pieces which once occupied the "fun point," but were edged out by new ones. Put in photographs of the Humor activities of your department.

These steps are only suggestive and not exhaustive. You need not limit your activities only to the ones listed.

Conclusion

Your putting Humor on the agenda is well worth the effort. Humor brightens the workplace and, in some cases, makes it more enduring. It enables the people to shed their ego, to find joy in work, to enjoy life and to respect and admire people nearby. Humor on the agenda leads to improved communications, better health, lowering of tension, and setling of discords, mature outlook, more creativity and enthusiasm, and above all, camaraderie.

Bibliography

Ace, Goodman. 1980. "Humor through Adversity", Saturday Review, New York: June 1980.

Allen, Steve. 1987. *How to be Funny*. New York: McGraw Hill.

Barsoux, Jean Louis. 1993. *Funny Business*. London: Cassel.

Blumenfeld, Esther and Lynne Alpern. 1994. *Humor at Work*. Atlanta: Peachtree.

Bonham. 1988. *Humor: God's gift*. Nashville: Bonham-Broadman Press.

Bradrey, P. 1957. *"The Joking Relationship in Industry"* in *Human Relations*, Vol. 10: 179–187.

Braude, Jacob M. 1963. *Speaker's Encylopaedia of Humor*. Mumbai: Jaico Publishing House.

———. 1964. *Treasury of Wit and Humor. Englewood* Cliffs, New Jersey: Trentice-Hall.

Copeland, Lewis and Faye Copeland. (eds). 1965. *10,000 Jokes, Toasts and Stories*. New York: Doubleday.

Covey, Stephen R. 1990. *The Seven Habits of Highly Effective People*. New York: Fireside.

Droke, Maxwell. 1956. *Speaker's Handbook of Humor*. Mumbai: Jaico Publishig House.

Duncan, Jack W. 1982. "Humor in Management", *The Academy of Management Review*. January. Birmingham: University of Albama.

Fahlman, Clyde. 1997. *Laughing 9 to 5*. Portland, Oregon: Steelhead Press.

Fuller, Edmund (ed.). 1942. *2500 Anecdotes for all Occasions*. Avenel, New Jersey: Crown.

Goodheart, Annette. 1994. *Laughter Therapy.* Santa Barbara, California: Less Stress Press.

Goodman, Joel. 1995. *Laffirmations.* Deerfield Beach, Florida: Health Communications.

Goodman, Ted. (ed.). 1997. *The Forbes Book of Business Quotations.* New York: Black Dog & Leventhal.

Hawkins, Paul. 1983. *Growing a Business.* New York: Simon & Schuster.

Hodge Cronin & Associates. 1986. *"Humor in Business," A Survey.* Rosemont, Illinois: Hodge Cronin & Associates.

Humes, James C. 1996. *The Wit and Wisdom of Abraham Lincoln.* New York: Gramery Books.

Irving, Gordon. 1980. *Take no notice.* London: STAR.

———. 1986. *Comic Speeches.* London: Chancellor Press.

Johnson, Eric W. (ed.) 1989. *Treasury of Humor.* New York: Ballentine.

Kumar, Dinesh. 2006. *Corporate Capers.* New Delhi: Response Book.

Kushner, Malcolm. 1991. *The Light Touch.* New York: Simon & Schuster.

Lawrence, Robert Setoz. 1968. *A Guide to Public Speaking.* London: Pan.

Laxman, R.K. 1977. *The Management of Management.* Mumbai: Vision Books.

Levine, Jacob (ed.). 1969. *Motivation in Humor.* New York: Atherton.

Moody Jr., Raymond A. 1978. *Laugh After Laugh.* Florida: Headwaters Press.

Myers, James E. (ed.). 1996. *Business Humor.* Springfield, Illinois: The Lincoln–Herndon Press.

Osgood, Charles. (ed.). 2003. *Funny Letters from Famous People.* New York: Broadway.

Paulos, John Allen. 1893. *I think, therefore I laugh.* New York: Columbia University Press.

Perret, Gene. 1989. *Using Humor for Effective Business Speeches.* New York: Sterling.

Ranganekar, Sharu. 1973. *In the Wonderland of Indian Managers.* New Delhi: Vikas.

Rao, J.R.L. 1993. *Vijynanigalodane rasanimishagalu.* Bangalore: Nava Karnataka.

Reader's Digest. 1997. "Towards more picturesque speech," *Reader's Digest.*

Ross, Bob. 1992. *That is a Good One!* San Marcos, California: Avant.

Seth, Suhel. 2003. *Shock and Awe!* New Delhi: Lotus Collection.

Sethi, Subhash C. 1994. *Humorous Jokes*. New Delhi: Crest.

Sullivan, Karen. 1997. *The Funny Book of Work*. London: Brockhampton.

Shourie, H.D. 2001. *The Funniest Jokes in the World*. New Delhi: Penguin.

Times of India. 2001. Gag Bag.

Vas, Gratian. 1996. *Politician Jokes*. New Delhi: Sterling.

Williams, Pat. 1940. *Winning with One-liners*. Deerfield Beach, Florida: Health Publications.

Zuck, Roy B. 1999. *The Speaker's Quote Book*. Grand Rapids, Michigan: Asian Trading Corporation.

Name Index

Subject Index

About the Author

K. Sathyanarayana is writer and corporate trainer based in Bangalore. He is also Joint Managing Director, Leonardo Engineering (Pvt) Ltd.

Mr Sathyanarayana has a degree in Mechanical Engineering and worked at Kriloskar Brothers Ltd. from 1958 till 1994 until he retired as Corporate Vice President, Human Resource Development. During his long tenure at the company, he was responsible for heading divisions like product engineering, and research and development.

He has developed a large number of managerial development programs and has written and presented many technical papers at national and international seminars.

Mr Sathyanarayana has written a book on the unique sense of humor of Mahatma Gandhi, and published a number of articles on the sense of humor of well-known personalities like Albert Einstein, C.V. Raman, Thomas A. Edison, and Swami Vivekananda, among others. His interests include teaching and horticulture.